WHO WILL STAY?

Building a House for the Presence
of God in the World

D. W. Hansen

Who Will Stay?
© 2022 by Dwight (D.W.) Hansen

Published by Grafo House Publishing, Guadalajara, Mexico
In conjunction with Jaquith Creative, Seattle, Washington

Hardbound ISBN 978-1-949791-72-3
Paperback ISBN 978-1-949791-70-9
Ebook ISBN 978-1-949791-71-6

To contact the author or inquire about bulk discounts for churches and
Bible study groups, visit h4mx.org.

Unless otherwise indicated, all Scripture quotations are taken from the
Holy Bible, New King James Version. Copyright © 1982 by Thomas Nelson,
Inc. Used by permission. All rights reserved.

Scriptures marked NASB are taken from the Holy Bible, New American
Standard Bible, Copyright © 1960, 1971, 1977, 1995, 2020 by The Lockman
Foundation. All rights reserved.

Printed in the United States of America
25 24 23 22   1 2 3 4

ABOUT HEART4MEXICO

Since 1998, our nonprofit organization *Heart4Mexico* has assisted in providing life-giving transformation to Mexican communities through practical, Christ-centered ministries. These include church planting, an orphanage for children, an accredited School of Missions, and short-term missions teams. *Heart4Mexico* serves as a fountain of renewed hope and second chances to those we seek to serve, and we strive to maintain trustworthy standards and provide life-changing outcomes that will impact these communities for generations to come.

If you would like to support national pastors, missionaries, and projects, you can find more information or make financial contributions at h4mx.org.

Email: info@h4mx.org
Phone (US): 818-388-4835

CONTENTS

SHOULD I GO
OR SHOULD I STAY?

I worked with the mission organization *Youth with a Mission* (YWAM) from 1980 through 1990, and it was a decade of travel, fun, and great adventures for God. I loved it. Our passion was recruiting and sending people all over the world with the gospel, and I traveled worldwide to preach and reach out to those in need.

The goal of any short-term missionary organization, of course, is *going* into all the world and preaching the gospel. That is the first part of the Great Commission that Jesus gave the church in Matthew 28:19-20. I still remember the catchphrases we would repeat:

- "Go means a change of location."
- "If you don't go, you won't grow."
- "Go unless the Lord says to stay."

There's nothing wrong with that, of course. But as time went by, I started to sense a change happening within my heart. I didn't just want to go, go, go. When I got to where I was going, I found myself wanting to *stay*.

You see, the structure of our program was focused on training young people for a few months at a time, which meant that once the program was over, we would say goodbye to each other and to the people we were serving on the ground. The only person who stayed was my wife, Mary Jo (she was stuck with me). But I always felt the longing to stay and build things for a more extended season. I wanted to develop deeper relationships and see people grow and mature as Christians.

Eventually we moved to Mexico, where we continued doing short-term missions. The more I learned about the culture and the country, though, and the better my Spanish became, the more I realized how few life-giving churches there were in this land. My calling to plant churches comes from those early experiences and feelings.

There's a famous passage in Isaiah where the prophet hears God ask, "Whom shall I send, and who will go for Us?" Then Isaiah replies, "Here am I! Send me" (6:8). It's a Bible verse that is often used to talk about missions.

I don't think God is just asking, "Who will go for us?" though. I think He's also pleading, "Who will stay? Who will build? Who will care for the sheep?"

Yes, missionaries should go into all the world, but they need to know what they are going there to do. The task is not just to preach the gospel—it's to make disciples. And to make disciples, we need a place that can contain them. That container, that place of safety and growth, is the House of the Lord.

> Who will stay? Who will build? Who will care for the sheep?

I am convinced that the true power of the gospel to change lives is found less in the *going* and more in the *staying*. That is, God's transformational work happens through the ongoing process of community: building, loving, discipling, laughing together, walking together, suffering together, growing together.

Going into all the world is good, but let's

go with the purpose of building strong, healthy communities of Jesus followers. That is where the power of God works best.

It's been several decades since we moved to Mexico, and I'm as convinced as ever that the world will see Jesus best in the church. I know there are many critics of the church, and they have their reasons and their stories. The church is not perfect, and it has a long way to go. But I still believe in it. More than ever, in fact.

I've written this book for up-and-coming leaders and for pastors who are called by God to pour themselves into building His church. Your work is not in vain: it is divine, it is beautiful, and it is needed.

I've also written this book as a thank you to those who have remained in the US and other countries and generously supported us with prayer, love, finances, and visits. Your "staying" has built not just your local church but churches around the world.

And finally, I've written it for every believer. You and I make up the church. With all its flaws and imperfections, with its potential and its promise, with its successes and its failures, we are in this together. We are building God's House, and it is a House for all nations.

I can't think of a better place to be.

CHAPTER ONE

CLOWNS AND PUPPETS
OR THE HOUSE

"**W**E'RE TIPPING OVER!" MY WIFE SCREAMED AS she covered her eyes and held on. The old school bus with forty young people inside could barely handle the rough terrain. The women—and a few men—screamed every time the bus tipped too far to one side. Dust billowed in the open windows, and we had to watch our heads with every bump.

But eventually, we made it to the village.

We arrived at the central plaza and began to invite everyone we saw. "Come and see the clowns, puppets, dramas, and more!" we announced over a scratchy portable speaker. Once a crowd gathered, the young people on our team mimed, danced, and performed shows for the kids. Then we closed with a testimony and a salvation invitation.

It was the eighties, and we were leading mission trips like this twice a year, which was always an adventure. For me, it was the reward of the journey. I have always loved travel and great adventures for God. I remember raising money for those trips, praying for months, crossing the border into Mexico, and overcoming many obstacles to preach in the mountains of Sinaloa, which was drug cartel territory.

That day in the village, we could feel the positive response to our visit. Everything worked well. The clowns didn't trip and fall, the puppets' mouths synced with the voices, the music was on key, and everyone smiled.

More importantly, the message was compelling, and the presence of God was so strong that many began to cry. Countless people responded to the call for salvation and committed to following Jesus.

When we finished our program, we began to dismiss the crowd. I noticed a sunbaked older man leaning against the wall, watching us leave with an expression of disappointment on his face. He was one of the people who had responded to the invitation to follow Jesus. I went over to say goodbye, and I extended my hand to him. "God bless you," I said, in my barely understandable Spanish.

He replied simply, "You are leaving already?" Then he added, "Who will teach us now?"

His words went straight into my soul.

Build a Better Container

That day, I began to think about Mexico. As a country, it has been on the receiving end of what I call Christian tourism. The love of adventure and travel, the nearness to the United States, and the open doors for ministry have brought many visiting ministers. Floods of evangelists, prophets, and preachers pass through the nation, and people respond to the call every time. They receive healing, are delivered, and commit to Christ.

After the events, though, the foreign visitors leave, and there is no one there to teach them. For those who are committed to following the Lord, it is challenging to build and maintain a healthy relationship with Him because they are often moved by every wind of doctrine. Their isolation from other Christ-followers can stunt their growth and leave them vulnerable to deception and lies.

I remember asking one visiting speaker about his church planting efforts. He informed me that they start churches, but they do not pastor them. I thought, *that is like saying we have babies but do not raise them.*

An evangelistic campaign or a team that comes for a few weeks and then leaves is fine as long as there is some way to keep and cultivate the results of the effort. Unfortunately, the lack of a solid structure to be able to disciple the entire nation has left us like a broken container that cannot hold the harvest. Our nets are torn or nonexistent as fishers of men, and we are losing the catch. The evangelist or ministry team must build a better container.

Jesus designed the perfect structure to receive the harvest that He knew would come.

Fortunately, Jesus planned ahead for this need, and He designed the perfect structure to receive the harvest that He knew would come. It's the church, which is also called the House of God. He told Peter, "And I also say to you that you are Peter, and on this rock I will build My church, and the gates of Hades shall not prevail against it" (Matthew 16:18).

One of the last things Jesus told His disciples before He returned to heaven was this: "Go therefore and make disciples of all the nations, baptizing them in the name of the Father and of the Son and of the Holy Spirit (Matthew 28:19)." We have become pretty good at the "Go therefore" part, but too often, we neglect to "make disciples." Evangelism without a church community might win converts, but it can't make disciples.

We're missing the container that Jesus told us to use.

Every Town and Village

When I see Mexico's small towns and villages with no church, I realize that the Great Commission is still not fulfilled in this great nation. I live in one of the smaller states in Mexico. There are over 2700 towns and villages here, yet there are very few life-giving churches.

Towns and villages are dynamic. Every day, someone comes or goes, someone is

born or dies, someone is married or bur-
ied. To make disciples, we must live among
the people we are serving. The evangelist
or mission team holding a meeting is just a
snapshot of a moment in time. If we establish a life-giving church, though, the community has a witness that is as dynamic and
alive as the town itself.

Stephen said in the book of Acts, "Our fathers had the tabernacle of witness in the
wilderness" (7:44). The word "tabernacle" refers to a dwelling place for God. In the same
way that the tabernacle was a witness to the
presence of God dwelling in their midst, the
church is a witness to God's presence in the
wilderness of this world. It's a safe place. It's
a place where people can meet with God and
learn from him—not just once or twice, but on
an ongoing basis.

God uses His House to reveal His fullness
(who He is). The apostle Paul wrote that the
church "is His body, the fullness of Him who
fills all in all" (Ephesians 1:23). That means
when you see the church, you're seeing Jesus
Himself.

This House is a wonderful sight to behold. Isaiah prophesied, "Now it shall come to pass in the latter days that the mountain of the LORD's house shall be established on the top of the mountains and shall be exalted above the hills; and all nations shall flow to it" (Isaiah 2:2). The House of God is a glorious mountain, and it is where the presence of God dwells and where the whole world can see His glory.

The best way to show Jesus to people... is to make disciples by establishing a healthy community of believers.

The prophet Ezekiel spoke about how the river of God, full of provision, flows from God's House. "Then he brought me back to the door of the temple; and there was water, flowing from under the threshold of the temple toward the east" (Ezekiel 47:1).

God does everything through His House. I have this phrase printed on the wall at my church: "If you want to see Jesus, go to church. If you want the world to see Jesus, plant a church."

How do we take Jesus to every town and village? Not just by preaching, handing out candy, and leaving. That's a good start, but the best way to show Jesus to people is to fulfill His whole command. It's to make disciples by establishing a healthy community of believers.

In other words, plant a church.

Discipled by the Church

When new believers are planted in a strong faith community, they naturally begin to grow and thrive. Have you ever heard the phrase, "It takes a village to raise a child?" in the same way, I think it takes a church to raise a Christian.

Between 1982-83, I had the opportunity to serve in a ministry in Hollywood, California. No, I was not trying to become a movie star—not even close. Our mission was to rescue people off the street, mainly young people who had run away to Hollywood with the dream of becoming a star.

In our ministry there, one of my coworkers was very condescending to me. He came off as believing he was superior to everyone, actually. One day, he introduced me to a visiting group and told them that I was his "disciple." My brain nearly exploded at the thought. I remember praying silently, "God, he is not discipling me, is he? There is no way I want to be like him!"

That got me thinking, though. *Well, who is discipling me?*

The answer was obvious: Christ was (and is) discipling me through His Body, which is His House. Through His House, Christ uses many other people to raise us up and help us mature. We should give honor to whom honor is due, and the honor for raising me goes to Jesus and His church. Who I have become and what I have accomplished isn't the result of one leader or pastor, but rather it comes from the grace of God and all the encouragement, teaching, correction, and training by countless people over the years.

In the same way, the discipleship work Jesus calls us to today is not about creating exclusive, hierarchical relationships where "disciples" must rely on leaders for every little decision. It's about creating a space where there is mutual encouragement, teaching, and growth happening all the time.

The church is a community of disciples: people who have chosen to follow Jesus, to learn from Him, and to be changed by Him. Therefore, the church is the best place and the best strategy for discipleship to happen.

As I look back over the years, I'm amazed and humbled by the role the House has played in our life and ministry. Our story is a good illustration of just how influential and powerful the church can be.

As I mentioned above, throughout the eighties, my wife and I served in a missionary organization. I traveled all over the world, teaching and promoting the Great Commission of preaching the gospel to

The church is the best place and the best strategy for discipleship to happen.

every creature. My fellow missionaries in the organization were my life. We served and suffered together, and it was all for the glory of God.

My greatest desire at the time was to attend a leadership school in Amsterdam that was part of the same missionary organization I served. The school was a once-in-a-lifetime opportunity that I could not waste, a chance to live in a missionary community and study leadership with people committed to taking the gospel to the world. The school accepted us, and we even purchased our airline tickets. But, strangely, neither of us had peace about going.

I was getting annoyed at the lack of confirmation, and when I told my wife, Mary Jo, we decided to pray all night until God spoke to us about what we should do. Mary Jo is sensitive to the voice of God, and after only half an hour of prayer, she told me what I didn't want to hear. She said, "We shouldn't go to the school."

In my stubbornness, I kept praying until late into the night, until finally, I decided to surrender my will to God. We weren't going to go to the school in Amsterdam.

I asked the Lord, "So, where do You want us to go?" I did not hear any reply. I had no idea what to do. We couldn't stay on with the missionary organization without a clear commitment to serving in a specific area, so we had to leave, and the only option was to move in with my in-laws.

At this time, I understood how King David felt when he wrote that God had put away his acquaintances far from him (Psalm 88:8). I did not have any friends, and I lived with my wife's family and their cats and dog. The change from being part of a dynamic community of world-traveling ministers with high-level, world-focused strategic plans to living in my in-law's basement was a real shock. No matter how often I prayed, God wouldn't give me any other directive. I began to feel that perhaps He had fired me. I kept doing what I knew I had to do every day, but I felt like I had no ministry and couldn't find my place. I felt like an orphan.

One day, Mary Jo and I went to McDonald's

for burgers, and I remember telling her that I had lost my vision. I had no idea what we were going to do. I mentioned a few options to her that I honestly had no interest in doing, and at that moment, she looked me in the eye and said to me, "You are a missionary, and we are going to go preach in Mexico!"

She was right. God had never fired me; He simply moved me to another place.

Of course, to make it to Mexico, I would need funding, and at that time, I was living hand to mouth. To give just one example, I drove an old 1969 Dodge truck that used to belong to a center for juvenile delinquents. When I got it, the entire thing was covered in cuss words scratched deeply into the paint, so I had to sand and repaint it. Naturally, a cat jumped onto the hood before the paint dried, so I had a "cat hair paint job," and you could see the foul words if you looked hard enough. The truck had a standard

"You are a missionary, and we are going to go preach in Mexico!"

transmission, and I still remember Mary Jo driving it. I could barely see her head over the steering wheel. So yes, money was a real obstacle!

I started looking for opportunities to preach and raise support from churches I knew. One church invited me to preach in their Sunday service. After investing a lot of time into sermon preparation, I drove the eight hours to their location, full of expectations. When I arrived, the pastor took me aside and asked if they could hire me as the youth pastor for the church. I was shocked since I had communicated that I would be raising missionary support for our move to Mexico. After informing him that I was called to the mission field and could not accept the job, he was so offended that he asked a stranger who was passing through town to preach in my place. He prohibited me from raising funds, but I still had to cover all the travel costs. I drove home totally defeated.

Upon arrival, I received a call from a close friend who was the pastor of a church with no more than thirty members, all from a low-income area. He asked me, "Dwight, how are you? Do you need money?"

I honestly did not expect much, but I answered, "Of course!" I was in no position to go to Mexico and desperately needed income.

The pastor told me that someone had left an envelope with money for me on the church podium. I remember thinking, *How much money could there be inside? Nobody in that church has money.* So, while we were both on the phone, he opened the envelope and began counting. "One hundred. Two hundred. Three hundred. Four hundred." There was a pause, and he stopped counting. He always loved creating suspense.

Awesome, four hundred bucks, I thought.

But he kept counting. After reaching eleven hundred, he paused again, causing even more suspense. Then he continued until he reached two thousand dollars.

Wow! Twenty $100 bills had been left on the pulpit of that sweet, blessed church!

In my euphoria, I asked him who had left all that money, and he candidly said that it must have been an angel because there was no one in the church with that much cash. Whoever it was, it was the provision of God. There was no way I was going to make it to Mexico with what I had.

After we gave our tithe on the anonymous gift, we went car shopping. Unfortunately, while looking for a new vehicle, the engine of that miserable Dodge truck blew a head gasket and died. We soon found a 1979 white Ford LTD with a burgundy interior for $1800, and that was the car we drove 2,350 miles— pulling a trailer—all the way to Mazatlán, Mexico, a small city on the Pacific coast.

Through all the financial tests, I learned firsthand the truth of what God spoke to Abraham: "In the Mount of the LORD it shall be provided" (Genesis 22:14). Without the House, I would have never been able to go to the mission field. It was not other missionaries who sent me; it was God and His church.

I learned the valuable lesson that we can go into all the world, but someone must stay in one place and show the glory of God in their local area. I was so thankful for the local church. They were the body of Christ: the hands, the feet, and the mouth of Jesus for me.

The House Is Always Being Built

If you've ever owned a home, you know there are a lot of work and expenses that go into being a homeowner. Things break or leak on a regular basis, and you have to fix them. You must weatherproof the roof and windows periodically. You need to cut the grass and maintain the flowers, bushes, and trees. You are always on the lookout for potential safety issues. On top of that, you might choose to remodel occasionally to better fit your needs or to stay current.

In the same way, the church is always being repaired, restored, and rebuilt. We can't assume it's perfect just because we love it or because we have good memories here. How could it be perfect? It's made up of a bunch of imperfect people, after all!

We don't gather together because we are

flawless people who have no sin, but rather because Jesus forgives our sins and breaks the power of sin in our lives. He changes us, and that changes the church.

Nowadays, it seems there is an all-out war against the local church. There is criticism over buildings, the church's organizational structure, the need for tithes and offerings, the style of worship, and endless other points. Some movements promote the idea of responsible autonomy or a natural community. They teach that it is not necessary to have structure, dismissing even the idea of having pastors or elders. Others say that the church is no longer relevant: "We should go to the lost and not insist that they come to us." Finally, some argue that we should meet exclusively in homes.

I know many of these people are sincerely trying to follow Jesus and do what they think is best for Jesus followers. Many have likely seen the failings of leaders around them, or they've become disillusioned with the concept of church. I don't mean to discount their experiences, but I do disagree with their conclusions.

Strongly, in fact. I believe one of the great needs of this world is that everyone would have a church, the House of the Lord, nearby.

Yes, there have been many mistakes committed in the name of religion. Some of them were unintentional failures by people who should have known better, and some were abuses of power by people who had no business leading in the first place. Those failures don't mean that the church is a doomed idea, though. They mean that we need to work harder at building the church that Jesus envisioned.

> We need to work harder at building the church that Jesus envisioned.

There's a phenomenon I've observed over the years. When people leave the church, they often seem to get together to complain and gossip instead of trying to improve anything. They gather in the name of their cause or their offense rather than Jesus. I don't see how that helps them or anyone else.

The church is the most beautiful, glorious, admirable, ugly, scary, and horrendous thing that exists. It is beautiful because God is present, and it is ugly (at times) because people are present. The human element makes the church vulnerable and fragile. There will always be a reason to criticize the church, but it continues to be the plan of God and the bride of Christ.

Does that excuse abuse or hurt? No! Quite the opposite. It means we must continually be listening, learning, and growing into the beautiful church God called us to be. It means leaders must be humble and wise, and it means followers must be humble and wise, too. Nobody is "off the hook" when it comes to the church. We are all in this together. The answer to the weakness of the church isn't to destroy the church, but to work together to be the church we all want and need.

No Lone Rangers

Many children of God live without a spiritual home. That is not God's plan, though. The Bible frequently refers to us in the plural because we are meant to be together, not alone.

We are not used to thinking this way, though. For example, I grew up in the United States, which created a culture of rugged individualism in me. My forefathers were pioneers who developed a nation on their own, after all. I was taught to be tough, self-reliant, a Lone Ranger. Maybe you grew up the same way, regardless of what country you come from.

This thinking makes it difficult to understand God when He speaks to "us." Often, when we begin to learn who we are in Christ, discover our spiritual gifts, and win victories in our lives, we keep thinking about ourselves only as individuals, and we forget that God is building us together into His House. Many passages of Scripture are not just for me but the whole body. For example, Paul wrote Ephesians to the church at Ephesus in the plural, but often we interpret it as written to just one person (me, of course!) when we read it.

I vividly remember being in a small town in Chihuahua, Mexico, in 1983, and a certain pastor was ministering in a church where we were staying. The pastor was a great man of God, but his wife was pregnant and sick. After seeing the pastor's situation, I knew it was the perfect opportunity to start an incredible, world-famous, evangelistic healing ministry. So, I began to cry out to God, "Father, use me to bring healing to this man's wife."

I heard the voice of God respond to me like never before. He replied, "No! I will not use you."

I felt so bad after hearing this response, and I dared to ask, "Why Lord?"

God said, "I don't just want to use you. I want to use all of you." At that moment, I understood that we are one body, and He is the head. We began to pray as a group, and the Lord healed the pastor's wife. God received all the honor for her healing, and we all participated. Just as it should be.

> God said, "I don't just want to use you. I want to use all of you."

There are no Lone Rangers in the kingdom of God. Even though some leaders get more attention or seem to have more influence, they are only one part of the church, and their influence is a result of the community behind them.

God is not looking for individuals to stand out among the others; instead, He is looking for a body, a church, that can be His House. We must always remember that we are part of something that includes us but that is bigger than us.

CHAPTER TWO

THE PURPOSE OF JESUS

...on this rock I will build my church, and the gates of Hades shall not prevail against it.

—Matthew 16:18

"**L**ORD, WHAT IS MY CALLING? WHAT DO YOU WANT me to do?" I asked those questions many times when I started out in ministry. It seemed like everyone else was called to some exotic place or even to "all the nations." Their lofty titles, once-in-a-lifetime opportunities, and exceptional talents intimidated me.

I continually struggled with my identity and calling. Why was I here on this planet, and what should I do? Whenever I asked, the only thing that came to my mind was to preach the Word. *He calls everyone to do that*, I thought, but I decided that was a start.

Working in Hollywood in a rescue ministry as a young man, I finally got my chance to preach.

"We want you to speak to the guys off the streets four times a week," the director told me.

Since it seemed to be my calling, I accepted the challenge. My first opportunity was to preach three messages in one day. I studied, prayed, and even fasted in preparation.

Unfortunately, my first message bombed. It felt like the words coming out of my mouth fell to the ground. The second message was even worse. Several of the guys fell asleep!

My only hope was to redeem the day by hitting a home run with my last message. I looked out at the guys in the third meeting and gave them everything I had. I pulled out every story I could think of, shouted, acted out the parts, and did everything possible to communicate well.

Again, I failed miserably.

At that point, I knew what it felt like for the apostle Paul when, during one of his lengthy sermons, a young man fell into such a deep sleep that he tumbled out of a window—and died! The story turned out okay because Paul prayed for him, and he came back to life. But still, I can imagine Paul must have felt at least a little embarrassed that his preaching had put the young man to sleep in the first place.

When I finished preaching that third message, I felt like a total failure; God had called me to preach, but I couldn't do it. What a horrible crisis of identity. I was no good at the thing I was called to do.

Why even preach? I asked myself. *Do we just speak to speak? Is it just an opportunity to show people how much I know? What is the purpose?*

Often, we make the purpose too much about us. That's what I was doing. We make everything about our ministry and our calling. I wanted to know what God called me to do, but I never thought about what *He* wanted to do. I sought my purpose but did not seek to fulfill His purpose.

A purpose-driven life should be a life driven by *His* purpose.

Jeremiah the prophet told his friend and helper Baruch not to seek great things for himself (Jeremiah 45:5). Why? Because selfish ambition always produces evil things. James wrote, "For where envy and self-seeking exist, confusion and every evil thing are there" (3:16).

Too often, we do so much work for God but very little work with God. We define our mission, vision statements, and strategies without considering His ministry. He is building something, and we should help Him fulfill His wildest dream, not just ours. A purpose-driven life should be a life driven by *His* purpose.

I Will Build

How would you define the purpose of Jesus? If you could ask Jesus what He wants to accomplish, what would He say? Would He answer that His goal is to have many people believe in Him? Or that He wants everyone to be happy and just get along? Or that He wants to have an army that forcibly declares Him king? Or that He wants to put an end to this world and all of its evil?

We love to tell Jesus our deepest desires and biggest dreams, but do we want to know His? We need to strive to understand His plan and know His desires. He deserves a people who understand His heart.

When I was learning Spanish, they taught

me that the use of the future tense is often more forceful in Spanish than in English. It's a declaration: I will go, I will do it, I will be there. Worship songs often use this verb tense: I will worship, I will sing, etc. It is a statement of will, intent, and commitment. For that reason, Jesus gets my attention when He declares, "I will build My church." He will build His church, and the enemy cannot stop it. It's His will and His promise, and that needs to be taken seriously.

Jesus taught about the House, prayed for the House, and invested His ministry in the core leaders of the House.

Jesus is all about the House. It is more than a cute idea or another way to serve the Lord. It is God's plan. Jesus taught about the House, prayed for the House, and invested His ministry in the core leaders of the House.

Jesus often taught about the kingdom of God in parables and preaching. It was a common theme of His ministry. I've heard many people say that the purpose of Jesus is to build the kingdom of God. They say that we just need to proclaim the kingdom of God to all the earth.

I agree that we need to preach the kingdom, but I also know that the House is where the King dwells among us. If we're going to tell people, "The kingdom of God is here," where are we going to point them? The tangible expression of the kingdom of God is the community of faith. It's the disciples who are known by their love (John 13:35). It's the church. That's why I have a hard time understanding how someone can be in the kingdom of God and not be in a local church.

God's commitment to building His church is illustrated in the Old Testament by King David and Solomon. King David wanted to build a temple for God, but God told him, "Nevertheless you shall not build the temple, but your son who will come from your body, he shall build the temple for My name" (2 Chronicles 6:9).

So, David prepared materials and commanded his son, Solomon, to build the temple. David is an illustration of our Father in Heaven who gave his Son to build the House.

Solomon knew what his father's heart was. He said, "Now it was in the heart of my father David to build a temple for the name of the LORD God of Israel (1 Kings 8:17)." Solomon had a clear purpose. He had a mission entrusted to him by his father, and he knew what was in his father's heart.

Do you know what is in your Father's heart? Do you know what God wants to build through you?

Christ came to establish the House, and He lives to build it. Like Solomon, He knows His Father's heart. He has a clear mission and purpose.

I don't think it was a coincidence that Jesus was a carpenter. Carpenters are always making something. They spend their time gathering materials, planning out projects, gathering the right tools, and carrying out the work. In the same way, Jesus is a builder, and He is always making something. That "something" is a lot more significant than a dresser or a bed frame, though—it's the eternal church.

Filled with His Glory

The book of Exodus mentions a man who could also be considered a type or illustration of Christ. His name was Bezalel, and God filled him with wisdom and understanding to complete the task of building the tabernacle (Exodus 35:30-31).

Like Bezalel, Jesus Christ has the wisdom and understanding to build His House. As Christ continues to move among us, everything He does contributes to the construction of a temple where the presence of God can be made visible here on the earth.

Christ did not simply come to add converts to His new religion. He is not the promoter of a creed or doctrine. He is not selling something pretty. He is not a motivational speaker trying to better your life. He is not a politician. He doesn't run a social club. He is not trying to add more friends to His social network. Jesus's work, simply stated, is to build up believers so they can be a temple for the presence of God on the earth.

Throughout history, God has always created

ways to dwell among His people. After Israel left Egypt, God commanded Moses to make a dwelling place for Him in the wilderness as they traveled toward the Promised Land. "And let them make me a sanctuary, that I may dwell among them (Exodus 25:8)."

The people gave sacrificially to build a tabernacle, and when they had finished, the glory of God so filled it that no one could enter, not even Moses. The cloud would rest on the tabernacle until it was time for Israel to move, then the children of Israel would follow the cloud of His presence. The House (tabernacle) was the center of God's people; it was the place to meet with Him.

The temple that Solomon built was listed as one of the seven wonders of the ancient world by St. Gregory of Tours. When the construction of the temple was complete, the Bible says that the glory of God filled the temple, just like it had filled the tabernacle.

Many years later, Jesus came and began building the church. He did it all according to God's plan, even giving His life for the church. Jesus instructed His disciples to wait in

Jerusalem until they had received power from heaven. When they were together, praying in an upper room, the same glory that fell on the tabernacle of Moses and the temple of Solomon filled their meeting place.

Because Jesus fulfilled the plan of the Father, wherever two or more gather in His name, He is among them, and His glory fills the House of the Lord again. The prophet Habakkuk wrote, "For the earth will be filled with the knowledge of the glory of the Lord, as the waters cover the sea" (2:14). God wants to fill the earth with His presence, and His church is the container that receives and pours out His glory.

This is our calling as Christians: to be a dwelling place for God on the earth. The world urgently needs to know God's love and grace, which means they need to see that love and grace at work in us.

> This is our calling as Christians: to be a dwelling place for God on the earth.

Paul wrote this in his letter to the Ephesians:

> Now, therefore, you are no longer strangers and foreigners, but fellow citizens with the saints and members of the household of God, having been built on the foundation of the apostles and prophets, Jesus Christ Himself being the chief cornerstone, in whom the whole building, being fitted together, grows into a holy temple in the Lord, in whom you also are being built together for a dwelling place of God in the Spirit. (2:18-19)

I love the phrase, "no longer strangers and foreigners." I have lived most of my life as a foreigner in Mexico. After a long time, I finally became a citizen, but many still view me as a foreigner. For a while, I tried to disguise my appearance. I bought a sombrero and even some cowboy boots, but there was no way I could hide my blue eyes and my accent.

I might not always appear to fit in here in Mexico, but I'm so glad I "fit in" with the Body of Christ. I am not an outsider. I belong to the

House of God, to His family, and I am no less worthy than any other member. I am a vital piece of the whole body working together, and so are you.

The rest of this passage talks about how Christ accomplishes His purpose. He first lays a perfect foundation, and then the entire building grows into a temple made holy in the Lord. We are the material that Christ uses to accomplish His purpose. We are members of His household.

The final phrase sums up the result of this building project: we are "built together for a dwelling place of God in the Spirit."

That is our calling. To be a dwelling place for God, a holy temple of the Lord, a family, and a house for His presence.

Freeing Jesus

If the church is the container for God's glory, that means we have a big responsibility. God depends on us to be the church where His glory can dwell.

A friend of mine once told me, "Jesus Christ is a prisoner."

Almost offended, I replied, "That's not true! God is all-powerful and a prisoner of no one!"

The person responded, "If His body will not move, it paralyzes whatever Jesus wants to do, making Him a prisoner in His own body." My friend reminded me that God had chosen His House, and His House is His body. If the body of Christ is not present, then there are no hands to do the work and no mouth to announce the good news.

As Christians, we often cry out for God to "set us free," but we should pray that Christ would be set free through us, His church. The House is the fullness of God in the world. When we establish a living church, we set Christ free to walk and work in His creation.

Jesus will build His church, just as He promised. He is building it already: through each one of us, because *we are the church*. His glory is seen among us wherever we gather together and whenever we act in unity. His grace flows through us and into a world that urgently needs more of Him.

CHAPTER THREE

THE PLAN

Then you shall erect the tabernacle according to its plan which you have been shown in the mountain.

—Exodus 26:30 (NASB)

"READING ARCHITECTURAL PLANS" WAS BY FAR MY favorite class in college. I learned that some plans are made exclusively for plumbing, others are for structures, and so on. There are symbols for each item the design calls for in the building, from toilets to electrical outlets. You have to know how to interpret each one to read the plans.

In the same way, God has given us a plan, an exact schematic, a blueprint, to build His temple. The House of the Lord is His House, and as we labor together with Christ to build it, we should follow His plan and fulfill His desires.

Paul wrote, "For we are God's fellow workers; you are God's field, you are God's building. According to the grace of God which was given to me, as a wise master builder I have laid the foundation, and another builds on it.

But let each one take heed how he builds on it" (1 Corinthians 3:9-10). We need to study and understand the plans for the House before we begin to build.

In 1999, I was worshiping on the front row of a church in Everett, Washington, while a preacher named Tim Bagwell prayed for more than 300 children he had called forward for prayer. The presence of the Lord was so sweet that I just stood in the audience, eyes closed, hands lifted. Out of nowhere, someone tugged on my tie and pulled me forward. It was the preacher. He brought me up to stand with the children, then he took a few steps back and looked at me. He didn't know me or what I did, but he began to speak to me. "There is a building ready for you... You need to step out and find it... When you return home, you will find a building for the church."

As soon as I returned, I gathered our team and said, "There is a building ready for us. Let's go find it." We didn't have any money, so they were astonished at my confidence. We had a promise, though.

So, we set out to look for a building. We

visited a few places, but nothing looked possible. It's tough to buy something without any money or credit.

Then a team member told me that "La Fuente," a venue that operated as a restaurant, bar, and event hall, was for sale. I was immediately intrigued because we were familiar with the building. We had even rented it for our Christmas program. I thought it would be too expensive, but I arranged a meeting with the owner anyway. To my surprise, he wanted the equivalent of $200,000 US, far less than I expected.

I offered to give him $15,000 as a down payment and pay the balance off in a year. The owner was so offended by my offer that he stormed out of the meeting. That day I learned several new curse words in Spanish! Naturally, I assumed that the deal was dead.

Even though I figured the owner was mad at me, I sought out some counsel. "You need to sweeten the deal," a close friend and counselor told me. Sure, easy for him to say.

A few days later, I sweetened the deal. I told the owner, "We'll give you $30,000 down and $2,000 a month for one year. Then we'll pay off the balance."

What I didn't know at the time was that the owner was paying $1,600 a month in interest on the building, and he was desperate to get out. To my amazement, he said, "Okay."

I stood there looking at him for a second, not believing that he had accepted the offer. The only problem was that we didn't have the $30,000 I had just offered him. "Just give us a few weeks to get the down payment together," I requested.

He agreed to that. "One more thing," I said, "If we buy your building, we want the name also." We had always wanted to name our church La Fuente ("The Fountain," in Spanish), but this restaurant/bar and event hall was already using that name, and we hadn't wanted to cause confusion, so we had named our church Centro de Vida ("Life Center"). He agreed to that, too. So, we bought the building and the name at the same time! It was a dream come true.

That was just the beginning of the miracles, though. Our 200-member church in Tepic gave $20,000 in one night in the first offering we raised, and we were able to pay the down payment. During the following year, we raised half of what we needed to buy the building, and a friend of our church graciously loaned us the rest. Within three years, this loan was paid off, and we owned the building free and clear. I am still amazed by God's faithfulness in that season!

If we were to operate efficiently and with wisdom, we needed to follow a master plan.

I never imagined owning so much space. Right after we took possession of the building, we began remodeling. However, we had more enthusiasm than wisdom. One day, we decided to move a sixteen-foot-high sheetrock wall. With thirty young people and a lot of rope, we slowly began to pull the wall across the church building. It seemed like a great idea at first—until the structure weakened, wobbled, and started to give way. Everyone saw what was happening and scattered. Except for one poor guy. The wall fell right on his head. I was panicking, of course, but he simply broke through the sheetrock. Apart from the scare, he was fine.

After such a close call, though, I knew we could not just build on a whim. If we were to operate efficiently and with wisdom, we needed to follow a master plan.

God's Master Plan

In the same way, we must follow a wise master plan when building God's House. God gave a blueprint to Moses for how He wanted the tabernacle built. The children of Israel made it exactly according to that plan: "Thus all the work of the tabernacle of the tent of meeting was finished. And the children of Israel did according to all that the LORD had commanded Moses; so they did" (Exodus 39:32).

Because they followed the plan, the presence of God dwelt among them, giving testimony to His presence and power in the wilderness. "Our fathers had the tabernacle of witness in the wilderness, as He appointed, instructing Moses to make it according to the pattern that he had seen" (Acts 7:44). Likewise, when we follow God's plan, the church becomes a great testimony in the wilderness of this world.

The tabernacle was a symbol of the true dwelling of God, which is His church. The author of Hebrews wrote that the tabernacle and its furnishings were "the copy and shadow of the heavenly things, as Moses was divinely instructed when he was about to make the tabernacle. For He said, 'See that you make all things according to the pattern shown you on the mountain'" (Hebrews 8:5). In other words, God's specific design for the tabernacle was meant to reflect His specific design for the heavenly church, which is the Body of Christ. If He took great care with the materials and construction of a tent that traveled in the wilderness for a few decades, doesn't it stand to reason that He would take great care with the construction of His eternal House today?

When we look at the modern church, we often do not see the fullness of Christ. We see some good things, of course—we also find a whole bunch of problems. Now, the temptation is to blame the problems on a lot of different things. But the bottom line is that, in many ways, we are not building according to the biblical model. Our churches are full of rules, forms, and traditions that are not found in the Bible. We cling to the traditions of men more than the commandments of God.

Building the House on a whim is a bad idea, though—just like moving a sixteen-foot wall with ropes. Instead of walking in human wisdom, we need to learn what the Bible says about His House.

The Acts Blueprint

The book of Acts is a great model for the church. Every time I read Acts, I desire to see today's church living up to its calling and potential to impact the whole world. The early church wasn't perfect, of course, but it was a living, growing, holy, powerful, Spirit-filled, influential force for good. There are a lot of truths we can learn from the example of the apostles and the church they built and loved.

One of the clearest truths the early church demonstrates is *the power of unity*. Unity was not just a theory but a foundational part of the Christian life. The book of Acts states, "all who believed were together, and had all things in common," and they continued "daily with one accord in the temple, and breaking bread from house to house..." (2:44-47). Seeing people united in brotherly love as they walk with Christ is impressive.

A second truth that the believers in Acts demonstrated was *true encounters with the living God*. They lived in the presence of God, and they understood that the kingdom of God was among them. For example, one day, Peter and John went to church to pray, and on the way, Peter responded to a lame man who was begging: "Silver and gold I do not have, but what I do have I give you: In the name of Jesus Christ of Nazareth, rise up and walk" (Acts 3:6). The man was healed instantly.

Walking with Jesus is that simple. What they had, they gave. Jesus had told His disciples earlier, "And as you go, preach, saying,

'The kingdom of heaven is at hand.' Heal the sick, cleanse the lepers, raise the dead, cast out demons. Freely you have received, freely give" (Matthew 10:7-8). If you don't know what to do in ministry, start right there. Find a way to freely give away what you have received.

Each person in that first church understood that a genuine encounter with Christ was a requirement. They were not joining a religion but rather being born again into a living relationship with Christ. They were baptized with the Holy Spirit, which meant being filled with power and living in communion with God and their brothers and sisters.

Find a way to freely give away what you have received.

A third characteristic of the early church was their *commitment to the church.* This wasn't blind loyalty to an organization but sincere commitment to one another. From the beginning, they understood the importance of meeting together, serving one another, and doing life together.

When a couple comes to me wondering about divorce, I remind them of the commitment they made "for better or for worse." This commitment is what makes it possible to push through conflicts until they find resolution. That is why my wife and I never even joke about divorce. We promised, and we must overcome our conflicts. It is not an option to quit when the going gets rough. Instead, we talk, pray, learn, grow, humble ourselves, show grace, and work at it until we find healthy resolution.

In the same way, church communities will experience difficult seasons at times. There might be conflicts, offenses, and misunderstandings. If we have made a commitment to each other, though, and if there is true brotherly love between us, we will persevere. We will seek resolution. We will learn and grow until we become better people because of the conflict, rather than letting conflict drive us apart.

The fourth thing we learn from Acts is that the House of the Lord was founded on *the apostles' teaching* and not on the latest ideas or winds of doctrine. The apostles heard the words of the Lord Jesus Christ, followed them, and taught them to others. This teaching produced genuine change in the lives of the believers. They were willing to lay their lives down for God. We are a house built on the rock when we listen to His Word and do it.

Fifth, in Acts, we see *leadership by a team of elders acting in love*. The leaders did not serve from a motivation to make money but rather from the heart. When one man wanted to buy the gift of God, Peter rebuked him strongly (Acts 8:20-23). They were not professional clergy but servant leaders, called by God to do the work. The ministry was not a platform for their fame, a political power base, or a source of riches (although workers are worthy of their wages). They were a united team that loved one another, and each one offered the gift they received from God to the church. Apostles, prophets, evangelists, pastors, and teachers served the church as elders and built up the members of the body. In my experience, lousy church government is a common cause of division in the modern church. (We'll talk about that in a later chapter.)

Sixth, the early disciples devoted a lot of time to *prayer and worship together*. They were all together praying when the Holy Spirit filled the place. Peter and John were headed to the temple at the hour of prayer when the lame man received healing. The apostle Paul wrote much on prayer. Paul and Silas prayed and sang hymns in prison. The book of Acts is full of examples of people with a real, living relationship with God.

> We need God's wisdom and creativity to know how to apply His principles wherever He calls us to build.

Today, careers, education, and other commitments often interfere with the House of God, and our schedules are so full that regular church attendance can be difficult. Then we ask God why there is no power in our churches. We wonder why the early church experienced miraculous power and influence that we don't see today. The difference is simple: love for Jesus and each other was their first priority. That doesn't mean they neglected their other responsibilities, but it does mean they took their time together seriously.

Finally, in the book of Acts, *the presence and power of Christ* were manifested often. The power of God exploded on the day of Pentecost, touching neighbors, the state, the nation, and the ends of the earth. The whole world could see the reality of a church full of His power. "Then fear came upon every soul, and the Lord performed many signs and wonders through the apostles" (Acts 2:43).

As we have seen, Acts is a great model of how the House should be built. That doesn't mean it is a book of commandments we must follow to the letter. Some of their methods don't apply today because each culture and environment is unique, so we need God's wisdom and creativity to know how to apply His principles wherever He calls us to build. In our building process, the heart, passion, love, unity, and overall example of the early church are priceless. We need to catch the heart of their story and build with the same blueprint.

We don't need to build on our own, using human logic or experience. Instead, we can look to God's design. He has a plan, and the more we build according to that plan, the greater His House will be.

CHAPTER FOUR

THE FOUNDATION

If the foundations are destroyed, what can the righteous do?

—Psalm 11:3

W HEN WE HEARD THAT WALMART WOULD BE building a store in Tepic, we were ecstatic. It was the early nineties, and at the time, we only had two medium-sized grocery stores with limited products. For months, we passed by the land where the building was supposedly going to be built, but all we saw were heavy machinery and a lot of people playing in the mud. Then, one day, the walls were entirely up. I realized that all that time, they were working on the foundation. Once the foundation was solid, the work progressed quickly.

Whenever we build something, a large portion of the budget and time is spent on what goes underground. God took over 4,000 years to lay the foundation for His church, a foundation strong enough to support the House of God.

In Ephesians, Paul speaks about the

foundation of the House: "...having been built on the foundation of the apostles and prophets, Jesus Christ Himself being the chief cornerstone (2:20)." Notice the foundation has three parts: the prophets, the apostles, and Christ Jesus, the cornerstone.

The strategy of the enemy is to destroy the foundations. Often, he does this by attacking one of the three things above. In other words, people emphasize part of the foundation and neglect the rest. That leads to weakness and failure in the church because the entire foundation is important—not just one part of it. Let's examine each of these three parts in more detail.

A Three-Part Foundation

The first part of the foundation is the *prophets*. The prophets represent the Old Testament teaching. The law and the prophets were God's revelation to Israel before Jesus came in the flesh. The law is absolute, and there is no room for grace and mercy. That's why there was a system of sacrifices in Israel: because nobody could fulfill the entire law. Unfortunately, some people and ministries build only on the foundation of the law and prophets. They are legalistic and rule-based. In place of a living relationship through faith, they focus on following the rules.

I remember a fellow student in my missionary training program who was about ten years older than I was. He was the single father of a sweet little girl, but he was so legalistic. He was very hard on his daughter and on us, his fellow students. He would memorize verses about judgment, righteousness, and holiness and completely ignore anything about God's love and grace. He never learned to value a gracious, love-filled relationship with Jesus. Soon after completing school, he converted to Islam. He built the whole House only on the law and the prophets, and it did not stand.

The second part of the foundation for the church is the *apostles*, who represent the New Testament. Some churches are built only on the foundation of the New Testament. They ignore the valuable truths of the Old

Testament completely, focusing only on what they see in the teaching or example of the New Testament.

For example, there is a group of churches that does not allow musical instruments in their services because the New Testament does not mention using musical instruments in worship. It only speaks of singing and making melody with your heart to the Lord; therefore, they only permit singing. However, God already taught us how to worship in the Psalms. Everything that has breath should praise the Lord, and every available instrument should join in worship. Worship is taught so well in the Old Testament that there is no reason to repeat it in the New Testament.

The third part of the foundation is *Jesus*. Again, there are some who make this their entire foundation. They believe that Jesus is the "nice God" in the Bible, and they advocate only reading "the words in red." They are only building on a small part of the New Testament.

However, God inspires all Scripture. Paul wrote, "All Scripture is given by inspiration of God, and is profitable for doctrine, for reproof, for correction, for instruction in righteousness, that the man of God may be complete, thoroughly equipped for every good work" (2 Timothy 3:16-17). Loving people doesn't mean we reject the justice of God. We don't continue to sin so that grace can abound. We use all Scripture to build the House. We utilize the whole foundation.

These three parts of the foundation—prophets (Old Testament), apostles (New Testament), and Jesus—provide strong support for a healthy House. All three are necessary. The most important, though, is Jesus Himself. That's why the Bible calls Him our "cornerstone" (see 1 Peter 2:6-7). Nowadays, we have great tools for surveying and laying out a foundation. The methods have significantly changed since Bible times. Back then, a cornerstone was used to identify where the first corner of the building sat, and it was the defining point of measurement for the rest of the foundation

As our cornerstone, Jesus is the point we measure by.

and ultimately the building.

As our cornerstone, Jesus is the point we measure by. A good foundation is in line with Jesus, the chief cornerstone. He said, "Therefore whoever hears these sayings of Mine, and does them, I will liken him to a wise man who built his house on the rock" (Matthew 7:24). If one corner is out of line when building, you don't move the cornerstone. You adjust the crooked corner until it aligns with the cornerstone. If you move the cornerstone, you will be entirely out of line, and the house will suffer.

When a foundation or a wall is absolutely level and in line with the rest, we call it "true." Likewise, our lives are true when we are in line with Jesus. He is the truth, and when our lives line up with His teaching, we are true.

A House that Prevails

In the mountains of Sinaloa, people have a great fear of a phenomenon they call a tornado of water. This occurs when water is sucked up from the ocean and then dumped in one spot in the mountains.

This happened one day in a village where we had started a church, and it caused a terrible flash flood. The neighbor's house in front of us washed away because of its poor foundation. She lost her life, and the water took her home and everything in it. It was so sad. The water that rushed through the town dragged cows and other animals to the sea, to the point that the fishermen there were catching cows instead of shrimp.

> Nothing can overpower the House of God when it's built on the right foundation.

Similarly, the enemy comes in like a flood against the church because he knows that the best way to take us down is to destroy the House. "...when the enemy comes in like a flood, the Spirit of the LORD will lift up a standard against him" (Isaiah 59:19).

There is an all-out attack on the foundation of the House. The enemy knows that if he can destroy the House, nothing will stop him. I quoted Psalm 11:3 above. "If the foundations are destroyed, what can the righteous do?" Therefore, the strategy of the enemy is to destroy the foundations. If we do not build the House on the prophets and the apostles, it cannot stand. Even worse, when we reject the divinity, power, preeminence, or teaching of Jesus, we decapitate the body of Christ.

If the foundation of the House is strong, however, even the gates of Hades cannot and will not overpower the church. The enemy might come in like a flood, but he will not succeed. I have seen a river of evil that flows against the church. Every time we plant a church, the enemy tries to kill it before it is even born. But nothing can overpower the House of God when it's built on the right foundation.

I remember when we started the church in Tepic, Nayarit. We had great favor, and the church began to grow in the building we rented. The time came to buy some sound equipment and supplies, so we headed to Guadalajara, a large city two hours south of us. After purchasing the perfect speakers for our sound system, we went to Costco for one last stop before heading home. Our one-year-old truck was loaded up with the sound equipment and other purchased items, along with our passports and four hundred dollars in cash.

At Costco, we filled up two carts with the things we needed. When we went out to the parking lot, the truck was gone! I could not believe it. Someone had stolen my truck with everything in it. I quickly called the police to report the robbery. "What is the license plate number?" they asked. *Who memorizes their license plate?* I thought. So began the trial of my stolen truck.

I spent hours and hours replacing passports, filing police reports, and submitting insurance claims. It took a year to receive the insurance money, and in the meantime, I had to keep making payments on the truck as well as buy a small car. That, together with the costs of a new church, caused my expenses to far outpace my income, and I went into debt. The debt produced a heavy burden of stress and worry. It was over a year before God miraculously provided. We prevailed by the grace of God, but it certainly wasn't easy.

Sometimes the attack is internal, not external. That is, it starts within the heart or character of the church leaders. Around the time we started the church in Tepic, I saw a tidal wave of evil hit the west coast of Mexico. In just one year, at least one prominent pastor in every big city on the west coast of Mexico committed adultery. It was tempting to think that no pastors were faithful to their wives. Important churches throughout Mexico were divided and many people were hurt by the weakness of these leaders. Somewhere along the line, those pastors neglected the foundation of their own faith.

Each church we have started has to make it through various "startup tests," as I sometimes call them. I have seen waves of attacks against the church my whole ministry life, but I've also seen God's grace and power to resist the enemy and establish His House.

Truth, Love, Faith

There are several important realities that the foundation relies upon. These include the *truth* of the Word, the value of brotherly *love*, and *faith* in the church's role today. Let's look at each of these briefly.

First, our foundation relies on the truth of the word of God. Jesus said that the person who hears His words and obeys them builds on a firm foundation. Therefore, if the enemy wants to destroy the House of the Lord, he first needs to reject or twist the Word of God. When I hear so many people speak evil of the church, I ask myself if they have ever read the Bible.

I cannot understand how they say we do not need pastors or leadership when the Bible says, "And He Himself gave some to be apostles, some prophets, some evangelists, and some pastors and teachers" (Ephesians 4:11).

I cannot understand how they say that preaching is ineffective when the word of God declares, "How then shall they call on Him in whom they have not believed? And how shall they believe in Him of whom they have not heard? And how shall they hear without a preacher?" (Romans 10:14).

And I cannot understand how they say that meeting together is unnecessary when Hebrews encourages us, "...consider one another in order to stir up love and good works, not forsaking the assembling of ourselves together, as is the manner of some, but exhorting one another, and so much the more as you see the Day approaching" (Hebrews 10:24-25).

God adds people to the church, and we are called to love them.

The second crucial reality that our foundation relies upon is brotherly love. "Let brotherly love continue" (Hebrews 13:1). Sometimes it's easier to love a stranger or someone across the world than to love the brother or sister in the Lord who is right next to us. And yet, God adds people to the church, and we are called to love them. They are our first priority.

When I first accepted the Lord, the church I was attending seemed perfect, and all the Christians there were my heroes. I wanted to be in church every day, to the point where I even attended what we used to call the "old folks' prayer meeting." I did not concern myself with the church's problems. I was in my first love.

However, there was one guy who truly bothered me. He was the fly in the ointment, the thorn in my shoe. He started to irritate me more and more, but I had a plan of escape. I was heading to a missionary training school designed for people like me. He would be out of my life soon.

I remember arriving at the school, finally free from that guy for good. Excited to be on my new adventure, I went to my designated room in a small cabin for student housing. A fellow student sat on the bottom bunk, and it quickly became clear that he was ten times more irritating than the guy at my home church. He only talked about himself and complained constantly. He was the youngest student they had ever received, and he mocked me all the time for not being "cool" enough. It quickly became clear that the six months together in a cabin would be a great trial for me.

While reading a book called *Rees Howells: Intercessor*, I read, "I started at the bottom and loved just one; and if you love one, you can love many; and if many, you can love all" (Norman P. Grubb, Lutterworth Press, 1952)

Our Lord said it even better. "For if you love those who love you, what reward have you? Do not even the tax collectors do the same?" (Matthew 5:46). It is easy to love those who love you, but loving those who irritate you is quite another thing. The foundation of the House is the love we have for one another. Brotherly love is like the cement that goes into the foundation of the temple of the Lord.

My project in that school was to love just one, and I had to love my irritating roommate with brotherly love. I still remember one day complaining to God about him. "How can I love him? He is impossible. He is the one un-lovable person on the earth."

"Love gives" is all that came into my mind. So, using the last of my change, I bought a Snickers bar for him and left it on his bed. He gobbled it up in a second without a word of thanks or question about who left it.

The big test came when I put on my new tan corduroy three-piece John Travolta suit and looked in the mirror. "Give him your suit," the Lord said. So, I sacrificially gave it to him. Love always gives, and I can tell you that I loved him.

The third reality that our foundation relies upon is our faith that the local church is God's plan. The church isn't just one of many ways to do ministry—it's a God-designed strategy to reach people, love them, care for them, and teach them.

The work of the ministry is part of the Body of Christ because *each of us* is part of the Body of Christ. Our work and service are an extension of what Jesus is doing through the church in all its many forms. To claim that the local church is unimportant or secondary misses the point that we are all part of Christ's body and church, and we are in community and connection with one another. Rather than diminishing the church's

> The church has a unique calling to change the world.

role, we need to celebrate it.

For my wife and me, the ministries we lead or serve in are part of the House of the Lord. They are never separate from the House. For instance, we are not an orphanage with a church, but rather a church with an orphanage. We are not a Bible School with a church, but rather a church with a Bible School. All our ministries flow from the House. Isaiah said, "the mountain of the house of the Lord / will be established as the chief of the mountains" (2:2 NASB). The church is the "chief mountain," and it holds an important role in coordinating and empowering other ministries.

I'm not saying the church must control every ministry that exists. That's not possible or healthy. I'm simply saying that the church has a unique calling to change the world, and if we are not intentional about building the church, we won't see the fullness of God's presence and power on the earth.

The House that God is building is beautiful, and it deserves a strong, healthy foundation. A foundation built on the prophets, apostles, and Jesus Himself. A foundation that finds strength in truth, love, and faith. Paul put it this way:

For we are coworkers in God's service; you are God's field, God's building. By the grace God has given me, I laid a foundation as a wise builder, and someone else is building on it. But each one should build with care. For no one can lay any foundation other than the one already laid, which is Jesus Christ. (1 Corinthians 3:9-11)

I am convinced that Christ has laid the perfect foundation for His church, and His church will change the world. Our job, like Paul, is to build on that foundation. It will be a glorious House!

CHAPTER FIVE

THE WALLS

...in whom the whole building, being fitted together, grows into a holy temple in the Lord, in whom you also are being built together for a dwelling place of God in the Spirit.

—Ephesians 2:21-22

TO BUILD WALLS, YOU NEED MATERIALS. WHETHER you choose stone, brick, or wood, you must start with the raw materials.

The material used to build the walls in the House of God is you. "You also, as living stones, are being built up a spiritual house, a holy priesthood, to offer up spiritual sacrifices acceptable to God through Jesus Christ" (1 Peter 2:5). You and I are living stones!

People are the essential resource in the House. Many seem to believe that the essential resource we have available is money, but the truth is that human resource is the most important element in the church. Try to grow a church without people! It is impossible. It doesn't matter how much money you have or how fantastic your building is. If you lack the presence of God or people, you have nothing. The Bible says, "For where two or three are gathered together in My name, I am there in the midst of them" (Matthew 18:20).

We begin to build with the people God sends to the House: those He adds to the church. Scripture says that growth comes when we are "joined together" (Ephesians 4:16); in other words, when we are united. Another way to say this is "organized compactly." When we are united or close to one another, we form the walls of His church. The temple will not grow without you and your brother or sister. We are not alone in this. The English poet John Donne wrote the line, "No man is an island," and he was right. The Lord designed us to be connected. We are part of a great House that Christ is building, and we are the raw materials.

One of the first examples in Scripture of a group of people who were closely connected is the story of Noah's ark. For more than a year, God closed Noah and his family inside a giant boat with sample specimens of all the world's animals. "So those that entered, male and female of all flesh, went in as God had commanded him; and the LORD shut him in" (Genesis 7:16).

If you think it is hard to be close to some Christians, imagine how Noah's family felt. The noise of clacking, cooing, mooing, meowing, snorting, snarling, barking, and roaring would have been an endless racket. Add to that the smells, the seasickness, and so many other unmentionable things. I'm sure by the end of it, some of them were looking for a different boat.

My point isn't that being close together is miserable. It's not. It's life-giving! Sure, there are a few uncomfortable moments. Yes, you might need to give each other some space at times. But ultimately, the closeness and togetherness of a community are what keep it safe when the rains and floods come.

The Problem with Living Stones

Part of the concept of "discipleship" is this process of becoming organized compactly or well-coordinated within the body of Christ.

Like bricks placed on top of one another and cemented together, we form the walls, thereby becoming a container for His presence. God always brings us closer to our brothers and sisters because they are the stones God uses to build the House.

The problem with this system, of course, is that we are *living* stones. The material that makes up the walls is alive, which means it can run away. I'm joking (mostly), but it does happen. During the construction of the House, there are times that the process can be painful as the material is cut and fitted into place.

Imagine Christ building His church. He heads out in the morning dressed in His work clothes, wearing His tool belt filled with the tools He needs for His job. He has completed a perfect foundation, and He has a pile of living stones all ready to go.

Jesus proceeds to pick up a living stone named _____ (put your name here). Jesus examines the stone in His hand. As it is, it won't quite fit. But, as the master builder and the ultimate architect, He knows where to place the stone and how to cut it so that it can fit into its place in the wall.

Now imagine that when Christ raises His hammer to cut the stone, the stone yells, "NO!" And because it is a living stone, it jumps out of the hand of the master builder and begins to run for dear life. Jesus has to chase the stone down and convince it to take its place according to His master plan.

> Everyone benefits from the growth that happens when we learn to work together.

That mental image is humorous, but it's all too real. Being part of a community or family will always require some give and take on everyone's part. That is normal, healthy, and good. It would be unrealistic to think that finding your place in the House will be a perfect, pain-free process. You'll need to grow and change in your character, and so will those around you. Ultimately, everyone benefits from the growth that happens when we learn to work together.

When you begin to feel the discomfort of

being set into the walls of His living House, though, it might seem too hard. It could feel easier to give up. You might be tempted to say, "I feel like God is calling me to change churches." I have heard every possible excuse when God begins to require commitment from His people. The worst reason is the one that claims God is calling them to flee. Christ won't call you to flee from your place in the House.

Now, as I mentioned in the first chapter, there are instances where genuine abuse happens. I'm not saying you should remain in a place where you are in real danger. However, in my experience, many people leave their church not because they are being abused but because they are being challenged to grow, to change, to forgive, to love, to give, to be humble, or simply to get along with other people. In other words, they leave because that seems easier than dealing with their brother or sister in love and wisdom.

That's a problem. God's purpose is being carried out in and through His House, and if you are wondering what tools He uses to cut and form His stones, they are your brothers and sisters in Christ. "As iron sharpens iron, so a man sharpens the countenance of his friend" (Proverbs 27:17).

Your brothers and sisters are instruments of God. I have a brother named "Saw," a sister named "Hammer," and another brother named "Sandpaper." You probably do, too! They are always there, ready to go to work on the rough spots in my character. When Jesus shapes, cuts, and polishes you—using other people—how will you respond? Will you flee, or will you take your place in the House?

Talk It Out

Heather, a girl I went to missions training school with, was a nightmare. I grew up with three older sisters, but Heather was worse than any of them! I am the baby of the family, and I always enjoy making people laugh. But whenever I joked around, Heather never laughed. She only looked at me with disdain. All I ever perceived from her was disgust.

One day, I innocently went to the restroom,

and when I walked out, she said, "Uh, gross! We could hear you going pee. Don't you know that you should turn on the faucet so we don't hear you tinkle?" I couldn't believe it. All I did was use the bathroom. I even washed my hands! It impacted me so much that I developed a phobia of making noise in the bathroom.

My only hope was that the school year was ending soon, and I wouldn't have to be around her anymore. Sometime later, I spoke with the school director about being part of a small team he had planned for the following year. "That's great!" he told me. "Heather will be on the team too, and you can work together."

I almost had a heart attack. I told the director, "I'm sorry, but I can't stand another year with her. I can't be on the team. What else can I do?"

The director was sad because of my attitude toward her, and he replied, "Honesty is the best policy. You need to talk to her and clear the air."

The idea of talking with her filled me with dread, but I did not have any other option.

Trembling, I went to speak with her. I couldn't believe she had me so traumatized! I asked her what I was doing that irritated her. I told her that I felt terrible and asked her what I could do to change the situation so that we could work together in peace.

Leaning toward me, she said, "I'm doing it again. Every time I like a guy, I treat him like my mom treated my dad."

She apologized, and we ended up becoming good friends. Prior to that conversation, I couldn't understand why she didn't like me, but in reality, it the opposite was true: she *did* like me. But the pain from her past was affecting her actions toward me. Instead of believing and seeing the best, I judged her motives.

> For us to be united is the prayer and great desire of Christ.

When there is conflict, our first tendency is to run. We don't like conflict. We believe any lie from the devil, and we accept his excuses to not be in unity with our brothers and sisters. When we refuse to relate to one another, we are not building the house. Instead, we are hindering the work of Christ. He wants a church, and we make it grow when we love one another. For us to be united is the prayer and great desire of Christ.

The director of the school was right: the best response to conflict is honesty. It is speaking the truth in love. The Bible encourages us to "...[bear] with one another in love, endeavoring to keep the unity of the Spirit in the bond of peace" (Ephesians 4:2-3).

Loving People You Can See

It is easy to talk about unity when there is no commitment involved. We can talk in lofty terms about the unity of the church around the world, for example, or about our unity with other churches in our city. But that can be pure fantasy. Unity with people we don't even know is like loving a photograph. To be truly united with people, you must be in the House with them. You must be living stones, shoulder to shoulder, forming the walls of the House.

That is why the local church exists. Everyone speaks of the universal church, but too many hate the local church. If you can't love the people in your local church community, how can you say you love the universal church?

In Revelation, chapters two and three, there are messages for "the churches." These were directed toward specific local congregations. God saw these churches, knew their condition, loved them, and had a plan for them. In other words, He isn't just concerned about the universal church or individual believers, but about specific, local church communities, too.

Being part of the universal church without belonging to a local church simply doesn't work. You cannot submit to the King of the Lord's army without submitting to the sergeants and captains that He has sent. You cannot love God, whom you have not seen, and hate or ignore your brother.

By the way, not everyone who shows up at a Sunday service is part of the House that is being built. This building process is more than attendance, and it's more than just giving an offering or singing in the choir. The living stones who are being built into a House are those who are true disciples of Christ. They have united to accomplish the purpose of Christ, and they love one another with brotherly love.

God is building His temple. He is polishing stones and fitting them together, following His perfect blueprint, His master plan. Every brother and sister that commits to belonging to a local church forms part of the walls. The process isn't always easy, but the strength it produces is awesome and unparalleled.

CHAPTER SIX

THE COVERING

He who dwells in the secret place of the Most High shall abide under the shadow of the Almighty.

—Psalm 91:1

W ATER WAS EVERYWHERE, FLOWING THROUGH OUR church building in La Fuente Tepic. We had a river in our church, but it wasn't the river of God's presence! It was rainwater coming from the back room.

Eventually, we found the problem: a Coke bottle had somehow entered the drainpipe from the roof and plugged it, causing rainwater to leak into our building. That wasn't the only time this happened, either. The building had a great foundation and thick, high walls, but the problem was the sheet metal roof. When the gutters would get plugged by debris, water would end up pouring into the church.

The memory of that event reminds me of how vital a healthy covering is. We need protection from whatever could fall on us. Jesus is the covering of the House. He is the Head of the church. "And He is the head of the body, the church..." (Colossians 1:18). Jesus leads us, covers us, and protects us from everything the enemy wants to throw at us. We never want to get out from under His covering.

God Is Our Covering

"So, who is your covering? Who are you submitted to?" When people ask me this question, I cringe a little. I want to ask the person, "Well, who is *your* covering?" I'm tempted to say that my covering is the Pope or the archbishop of Canterbury. (Although, who covers the Pope?)

I understand the importance of not being Lone Rangers, living recklessly and without any sort of mutual accountability. However, Jesus is our covering, not another person or organization. A human being should never take the place of Jesus Christ in our lives. We submit to one another in love, but we are under the covering of our Lord.

What I've seen is that people often look for

someone to tell them what to do—and someone to blame when things don't go as they want. They give up their personal responsibility to make wise choices and instead expect another human being to be the Holy Spirit for them. That way, when things go wrong, they don't have to blame themselves. Their leaders become the target for their rage and frustration, scapegoats to blame for any failure.

What is it in humans that demands a visible covering, a king of sorts? We constantly want to be led by someone we can see rather than trusting the Head of the Body.

> Let no one cheat you of your reward, taking delight in false humility and worship of angels, intruding into those things which he has not seen, vainly puffed up by his fleshly mind, and not holding fast to the Head, from whom all the body, nourished and knit together by joints and ligaments, grows with the increase that is from God. (Colossians 2:18-19)

Israel demanded an earthy king, thereby rejecting their true King. "And the LORD said to Samuel, 'Heed the voice of the people in all that they say to you; for they have not rejected you, but they have rejected Me, that I should not reign over them'" (1 Samuel 8:7).

Israel wanted to be like the other nations. The Lord warned them that their king would take their sons and daughters, the best of their fields, vineyards, and olive groves, and a tenth of all the grain, sheep, and servants. Like Israel, when humans are the covering, we cry out for deliverance from their control and domination. Samuel warned them, "And you will cry out in that day because of your king whom you have chosen for yourselves..." (1 Samuel 8:18).

> Humans tend to look for an intermediary between God and us.

Humans tend to look for an intermediary betwen God and us. We are often too fearful and ashamed to go directly to Him. When God came down on Mount Sinai, the people asked Moses to go up, and they stood at a distance. "Then they said to Moses, "You speak with us, and we will hear; but let not God speak with us, lest we die" (Exodus 20:19).

In the same way, we often create a separation between the clergy and the laity. We draw a line between the sacred and the secular, dividing the priests from the people. That is a mistake, though. The Lord wants to walk with us, talk with us, know us—not just hear from our designated holy ones. We cannot delegate our relationship with Jesus to a chosen few who draw near while the rest of the people tremble at a distance. All of us are a chosen race, a royal priesthood, a holy nation, His special people. We are His inheritance. He earned us on the cross and is the only one worthy of covering us.

He is building His church, and He blesses what He is building.

Many pastors and leaders fall into a trap, trying to take the place that only Christ can have. After so many struggles with people who rebel and betray us, we can develop a Messiah complex. We hate the concept of controlling others, but we find it hard to avoid taking the place that only Jesus is worthy of occupying.

A spiritual structure that is based on head-on, direct orders rarely produces healthy relationships. If someone is your prophet and you receive God's word exclusively from them, you are no different than Israel sending Moses to talk to God on your behalf. What happens when the leader gets it wrong? We know that no human is infallible, and sooner or later, that person will fail you. You will be crushed and disillusioned by their failure.

We love people, yes, but ultimately, we put our *trust* in the Lord, not others. As David wrote, "Give us help from trouble, for the help of man is useless" (Psalm 108:12).

What does this have to do with the House? If you're in the House, you're under the shelter of the Most High. And if you are building the House according to His plans, you are building with the blessing of God Himself. He is building His church, and He blesses what He is building.

That means that a church community does give us "covering," in a sense, but not because we need another human to mediate between God and us. Rather, the covering is the result of God's glory and power caring for His people and for the work He is doing on the earth.

Here to Serve

We need to look at covering differently. In the kingdom of God, things are upside down. Leadership means service. If I provide leadership (which is what we often mean by "covering"), I must do it as a servant, upholding and edifying the church. Everything I say and do should be for the benefit of the people and the church, not out of self-interest. I provide, protect, and guide, but I must not lord it over those I serve.

Similarly, God's covering for us is not about tyranny but about blessing. There are provision, protection, and direction under the Father's covering. "He will feed His flock like a shepherd; He will gather the lambs with His arm, and carry them in His bosom, and gently lead those who are with young" (Isaiah 40:11). God has our back. He covers us like the roof of a great house, protecting us from the elements and dangers outside.

I've seen God's protection in our lives many times over the years as we have built His House. I remember one time in the early nineties, after a hard day of travel and a long, hot church service in San Ignacio, a tiny village where we were planting a church, a little girl came up to me. "Please come and pray for my father," she pleaded. "We think he will die."

I followed her down a dark, muddy trail to a house lit by a single light bulb, with pigs and dogs and several scared children all waiting for me out front.

God's covering for us is not about tyranny but about blessing.

It was creepy, to say the least. The man was lying on a cot, covered in sweat, with big, red welts all over his body. When I laid my hands on him to pray, I recoiled. He was burning up with a fever. I instantly understood why they said he was dying. I prayed for him. Then I left, telling them I would return and check on him in the morning.

In the morning, the place did not seem creepy at all. It was a small, lovely home full of sweet, smiling Mexican children. Still concerned for the man, I asked to pray for him again. "Oh, he is not here," they informed me.

"I thought he was dying last night. Where did he go?" I asked.

They told me that he felt fine when he woke up, so he went to work.

"You know that Jesus Christ healed him, right?" I said, "Where does he work?"

"He is a police lieutenant, and he is at the station right now."

Since it wasn't far, I went straight to the station and found him. He was in perfect health, and he was heading out on patrol. I asked him, "You know that God healed you last night, right?" He knew that the Lord healed him, so I asked him to come to church and give his life to Jesus. He promised to come, but he never showed up.

Months later, we were driving down a dark, windy, two-lane mountain road after an evening of services. I noticed the tiny beam of a flashlight directing me to stop. At the time, it was a lawless area known for drug cartel activity, and it was common for the police—or criminals—to stop people.

As I pulled to a stop, I saw it was the police. To my surprise, I saw them drag a couple out of the bushes on the side of the road and move them roughly to their car. The man was in shock, and the woman's clothes were ripped and covered in mud. I didn't know what was going on or what they were doing with that couple, but I realized we were in serious trouble. My wife, my baby boy, two other girls, and a couple of young men were in the truck with me.

Two of the police ordered us out of the vehicle to do who-knows-what to us. Just before we got out, the police lieutenant who had been healed came around the corner. He saw us and said, "It's those hallelujahs." That is a common, derogatory name for Christians. "Leave them alone. Let them go." He was the guy in charge of the band of police that was stopping people.

Amazed, we quickly drove home to safety and rest. That wasn't the last time the same lieutenant would come to our rescue in similar circumstances. The Lord healed him to protect His children as we worked to establish His House.

Who Has Your Back?

Not only is leadership about service, it's also about protection. The idea of "covering" that views leadership as ruling or lording it over someone is completely wrong. If we have been given authority, it is so that we can protect and care for those under our influence. That's what God does for us, after all.

Do you remember the scene in the 1992 movie *The Bodyguard* when Kevin Costner flies through the air and takes a bullet for Whitney Houston? That is the best way to describe our role as pastors and as friends. A bodyguard covers his client like a shield. He is willing to take a bullet for him. "Greater love has no one than this, than to lay down one's life for his friends" (John 15:13).

We see the concept of a bodyguard various times in the Old Testament. Often, this person was called an armorbearer. Their job was to make sure the warrior had every weapon they needed, when they needed it. It was to guard their back and protect them from unseen dangers. Armorbearers were also supposed to make sure the fallen enemy was dead. However, the champion was to get the credit for the kill. We need this attitude toward one another (without the body count, of course). We are here to protect each other, serve each other, and equip each other—and we don't care who gets the credit.

In Ephesians, Paul writes about the Christian's armor. If you read the list of armor carefully, though, you'll notice something: there is nothing to protect our backs. Why? First, because we should never run away in battle. In war, an old saying goes, "If I stagger, push me on. If I fall, pick me up. And if I run, shoot me." The second reason there is no back armor is that we have each other's backs.

> If we have been given authority, it is so that we can protect and care for those under our influence.

I am your bodyguard, and you are mine. And the third reason—and the main one—is that *God Himself* has our back. He is our covering and protection.

As I said earlier, the main covering we need is not another human: it's God Himself. He is our shield, our bodyguard, our defender. The prophet Isaiah wrote, "Then your light shall break forth like the morning, your healing shall spring forth speedily, and your righteousness shall go before you; The glory of the LORD shall be your rear guard" (Isaiah 58:8).

As we've seen, though, God's protection is found in a special way within the House. God builds, covers, and protects His church. As we align ourselves with what He is doing, and as we stay in relationship with our brothers and sisters in the House, we experience His protection. We watch out for one another, we encourage one another, and we empower one another. God's House is a safe place.

CHAPTER SEVEN

FILLING THE HOUSE

Through wisdom a house is built, and by understanding it is established; by knowledge the rooms are filled with all precious and pleasant riches.

—Proverbs 24:3-4

"DO YOU KNOW WHERE WE CAN FIND A CHRISTIAN church? We are looking for a pastor who lives near here."

It was the year 2000, and a missionary friend and I were asking the same question at each house in the area, trying to find a pastor we had heard lived in that small town in the state of Nayarit. We wanted to introduce ourselves to him, encourage him, and see if he needed anything.

Two helpful ladies informed us, "Yes, we know the pastor. That poor man lives in an abandoned house, but he has tuberculosis."

When we finally found him, he was just as bad as they had said. He was living in a tarpaper house and was very sick. He did not have any money to care for himself, and no one in his church could help. Of course, we helped him, but we left with a heavy burden.

We had a similar experience in a town in the state of Sinaloa. We found a man living with his ten children in a cardboard house next door to the church he pastored. Every day they dealt with dirt floors, scorpions, and sickness. An open sewer ditch in the church's backyard stunk up everything.

Such neglect shows how little value is placed on the House at times. There are many places where the House doesn't look very beautiful, and it doesn't compare to the church in the Bible. It is nothing like the glorious bride mentioned in Ephesians: "...a glorious church, not having spot or wrinkle or any such thing, but that she should be holy and without blemish" (Ephesians 5:27).

A Glorious House

To be clear, I know that some brothers and sisters simply do not have enough for their calling, and I would never criticize someone for being poor or sick. We all suffer at times, and we know that "many are the afflictions of the righteous," as the Bible reminds us. It's also worth noting that the early church suffered greatly, and they flourished in those times of affliction.

My point here is not that the church should be rich or never suffer need, nor am I talking about instances where financial lack or illness have created temporary hardship. Rather, problems arise when people simply don't value the church, or they don't see the church as beautiful, or they believe the church is somehow more spiritual or holy when it is suffering.

That doesn't sound like a glorious bride to me, though! The early church suffered, but they did not become a victim of their circumstances. They believed that God could make the church glorious in any circumstance.

Imagine the wedding feast of the Lamb. Jesus Christ, the bridegroom, is ready. All the angels are in attendance. We hear the wedding march begin, and in walks the glorious bride, dressed in fine linen, white and shining.

As you watch, though, you notice that she has a big stain on her dress: Apparently she spilled half a mug of coffee on herself just before the ceremony. Her hair looks like she just rolled out of bed. She is only wearing one shoe because she couldn't find the other one, so she is limping and clumping down the aisle like a hobbled horse. Her dress must have snagged on something because it has a giant tear in the hem, and wait—is that...a long strand of toilet paper dragging behind her?

We are supposed to love people and use money, not love money and use people.

What a nightmare, right? The bride of Christ should be glorious. But if we don't care enough to beautify the House, His bride will be lacking. God's House should have everything necessary to accomplish His will.

I don't know who decided that the church should be poor and miserable. Money is not the root of all evil. According to 1 Timothy 6:10, the *love of money* is the problem. In other words, the issue is greed. In the church, we are supposed to love people and use money, not love money and use people. Poverty is not a value of the church. One of the callings of the church is to help the poor, which means there needs to be enough funding to truly help. With wisdom, we will fill the House with good things.

By "good things," I don't mean wasting money on ornate, luxurious furnishings. I also don't mean lining the pastors' pockets with riches while the congregation suffers. I mean filling the House with what is necessary for it to function at full capacity. Just like a house needs furniture, dishes, electricity, water, and more in order to be useful, the House of God needs practical, tangible things to carry out its purpose.

That includes money, but it goes far beyond money. It means having the right people, the right equipment, the right building, the right strategies, the right talents, the right ministries, the right decisions, the right financial structure, and more. Above all else, it means filling it with the Presence of the Lord. If the House is to be effective, we must take seriously our role in "filling it" with all that is needed.

God's Plan for Abundance

As we fill and beautify the House, we must keep in mind that God's design for abundance is based on the generosity of people in the church. It's the tithe principle. This was clear even in the Old Testament, under the Law: "Bring all the tithes into the storehouse, that there may be food in My house" (Malachi 3:10). In the New Testament, there are countless exhortations to be generous, to give proportionally to our income, and to give regularly. A church that is satisfied with having too little usually reflects the poverty mindset of the members and the pastors, not the economic status of the congregation or the city.

I remember a pastor in our city who always seemed like he was in a bad mood. He complained nonstop about his money problems. "I don't have money to do anything," he would say. He complained about the stingy people in the church and said they couldn't afford a sound system or an extension to their building. They couldn't even afford to pay the electric bill. I suggested once that they hire a youth pastor, and he answered sadly, "How could I ever afford to hire a youth pastor?"

I know he saw me as a living, breathing dollar sign. Every time we spoke, that attitude was apparent. Finally, I asked him how he handled the finances in his church. He told me that the people tithed to him directly, and that was his salary. Any expenses for building projects or other needs required an extra offering because the tithe belonged to him.

That's a huge problem. The tithe belongs to God, not the pastor. Ten percent of all we earn should return to the Lord. That is the system that God left us to fill the house. Here's the full passage from Malachi 3:8-10.

> "Will a man rob God?
> Yet you have robbed Me!
> But you say,
> 'In what way have we robbed You?'
> In tithes and offerings.
> You are cursed with a curse,
> For you have robbed Me,
> Even this whole nation.
> Bring all the tithes into the storehouse,

That there may be food in My house,

And try Me now in this,"

Says the Lord of hosts,

"If I will not open for you the windows of heaven

And pour out for you such blessing

That there will not be room enough to receive it.

The storehouse is the treasury of the House. The whole tithe goes into the church's possession, and the church distributes it according to a budget set up by the leadership. Of course, the pastor deserves a salary; but he doesn't "own" the tithe.

I remember when someone once donated a refrigerator, microwave, and mini-fridge as an offering. A pastor suggested that we hold a raffle for the items, and that way, we could earn a lot of money. We made tickets and began to promote the raffle. It's tough to sell things in the church, though—it just didn't feel right. After several weeks we had only sold one ticket. I had to talk to the individual who bought the ticket, return their money, and apologize.

After that, I changed my mind entirely about selling things in the church. I know that some churches sell tamales, hold fairs, and more. It's not my place to criticize, but I don't believe anything can replace the system God created: generosity. "Give, and it will be given unto you," Jesus said (Luke 6:38). When managed correctly, we can fill the House with many things.

How to Fill the House

What can we do to fill the house with resources, people, and the Presence of God? While there are many things that could be mentioned here, I want to highlight three keys that have helped us fill the House.

The first and most important thing is *love and unity*. People will fill the House if there is love. Think about how powerful love is. Movie theatres are jam-packed with couples watching love stories. Countless songs extol the joy and heartache of love. There are endless books written on love. Websites rake in cash promising to help you find your "forever" match. Products of all kinds use love in their advertising.

Why? Because love is attractive, and above all, people desire to be loved. The attraction of a church should be that it is a place where we find true love.

The unity that fills the House must be true unity. As a pastor and leader, unity begins in my home: with my wife, kids, and me. If I am not in harmony with my spouse, how can I manage the House? Unity must include my staff and team of volunteers, too. As the senior pastor of La Fuente Ministries, my priority is to guard the unity among the team of pastors. If we are not in agreement, we cannot move forward.

Disagreement is not something to be ignored or overruled but rather listened to, discussed, and taken seriously. Coming to an agreement on difficult topics is not easy, but the process itself creates a bond of relationship and trust. Then we move forward together, learning and listening to each other along the way. There is safety and joy in knowing we are doing things as one.

The goal of unity is to be of one mind. "Nevertheless, to the degree that we have already attained, let us walk by the same rule, let us be of the same mind" (Philippians 3:16). The "same mind" means knowing what the other is thinking and acting together, with the same values and goals. Like a great sports team or a unit in the military, the goal is to be so united that we function as one body. To achieve that, we must learn how to get in agreement, walk humbly, and submit to one another in love.

The second key that fills the House is *faith*. Significant steps of faith lead to a full House.

> The goal of unity is to be of one mind.

I remember we didn't have anyone to play the bass guitar in worship in the early days, but I went to the store anyway and bought a bass. I set it down on the stage by faith, and in two weeks, we had a bass player. We began to pay a youth pastor when we didn't have enough money for it, and the money came in.

I'm not promoting irresponsibility, but rather calculated steps of faith. If you know where God is leading you, don't wait until your bank account is full. Take the first step, and trust God to provide the resources as you go along.

In 2 Kings 3, we read a story about three kings who went out into the desert to fight against Moab. When they ran out of water, the king of Israel was afraid, but the king of Judah had the sense to ask if there was a prophet of God among them. The prophet Elijah was summoned. Here's how verses 16-17 describe it.

And he said, "Thus says the Lord: 'Make this valley full of ditches.' For thus says the Lord: 'You shall not see wind, nor shall you see rain; yet that valley shall be filled with water, so that you, your cattle, and your animals may drink.'"

They learned a great lesson in faith that day: dig a ditch! If there is nothing, prepare to receive it anyway. That is how people of faith take steps of faith. As a result, the House grows in faith.

I remember when I was twenty-three years

old, I had a minor crisis. At the time, I was leading the Discipleship Training School for YWAM in Los Angeles. I had too many leaders making demands I could not meet. No matter how much work I did, it seemed like I could never get ahead of it all. I felt exhausted and incapable. I thought about people who had lived with great responsibility, and I asked myself how it was possible.

One day, I read in Psalms, "Unless the LORD builds the house, they labor in vain who build it; Unless the LORD guards the city, the watchman stays awake in vain" (Psalm 127:1). I remembered it was not my house; it was God's House. It is my job to walk in faith, and it is His job to fill the House. That lesson has stayed with me all these years.

The third key that fills the House is *fine-tuning* or "tweaking." We never graduate, we never arrive, and we never settle. Instead, we constantly ask, is the message clear? Do new people feel accepted? Have we developed weird religious habits?

The church is a living, growing organism. That means it changes all the time. We need a habit of constant, positive analysis of our operations. We must embrace change, not hide from it. This includes prayer and listening to God, of course. But it also includes study, research, and education. It includes looking to other churches and organizations for examples and ideas. And it includes experimenting to see what works in our particular environment.

> We must embrace change, not hide from it.

For better or for worse, I have a habit of trying to improve our facilities. I remember when we were remodeling our new building in Tepic, there was a small, basically useless balcony on one wall that bothered me to no end. We dug and moved dirt for a week to reconfigure our auditorium, and the process was going well—but that dumb little balcony was always there, taunting me.

It became a personal vendetta of mine to remove the eyesore. So, I rallied an army of volunteers, and we pounded with sledgehammers and even a jackhammer for days, with no success. The thing was made of heavy rebar and concrete. I believe they designed it to support an elephant.

Finally, I stood on the balcony. Looking down, I could see the main bar holding the whole thing up. I had an idea. *I'll just cut this bar, then move to the side at the last second, and let it fall,* I thought. *What could go wrong?*

So, like other distracted, overly confident builders have done, I used a grinder to cut the bar that was holding me and the tons of cement up! It is too bad no one was filming. That "fail" video would have gone viral for sure. When the balcony came crashing down, I fell ten feet backward to the ground, and my foot got caught in the structure. My foot was hanging there like a dead fish. I broke every bone and pulled every tendon in my ankle.

For ten weeks, I was held together with screws. It was a heavy price to pay for a slight improvement, but I learned a great lesson about safety in construction—and I defeated the balcony. To this day, I haven't stopped tweaking things. I'm just smarter about how I do it.

It can cost us a lot of extra effort to change, but without change, we will die. Churches need to adopt new technologies and methods all the time because everything changes quickly as knowledge increases. Cultural changes that come quickly can overwhelm a stuck or lazy church leader.

I've heard that some sharks must keep swimming in order to breathe and stay alive. I don't know much about sharks, but I do know that a church that stops moving forward will stop breathing and eventually die.

We can never stop growing and adding to the House. "We never graduate," "Numbers count," "Brick by brick," and "Until it's finished" are slogans that we use to communicate that we never finish the job of filling the House.

Through God's grace, diligence, and understanding, we labor together with Christ, filling the House with everything necessary to carry out God's plan.

CHAPTER EIGHT

ORDER IN THE HOUSE

Let all things be done decently and in order.

—1 Corinthians 14:40

YEARS AGO, WHILE SERVING ALONGSIDE TWO OTHER pastors in Mexico, the founding pastor had a vision. In it, he was trying to climb a mountain, but he could not reach the summit until two others came alongside. Together, they then reached the top. The pastor shared the vision with the other pastor and me, and he said he wanted to form a leadership team of three pastors with equal levels of authority to climb that symbolic mountain. I have always believed in working as a team, and I was fully on board with this plan.

At first, it went exceptionally well. The main church developed very quickly. We planted five churches north of the city and opened thirty home groups. We grew to over seven hundred people in attendance on Sundays. But the confusion caused by creating a three-headed monster caused insurmountable problems. Everybody wanted to be the director and leader, but no one wanted to serve. If someone asked one of the three pastors for something and the pastor said no, they would just ask the next pastor until they got permission. People constantly compared the pastors and competed for their favor, and it filled the house with confusion and disorder. We attempted to fix the three-headed-church problem, but we could not. Everyone had their favorite pastor, and they just got angry when we tried to establish the correct order.

The House cannot flourish if we allow confusion and strife to have a place. "For God is not the author of confusion but of peace, as in all the churches of the saints" (1 Corinthians 14:33). If we do not deal with disorder in the House, we will produce negative results.

To establish order in the House, someone has to lead. We know that in the home, in business, in school, and in politics, healthy leadership is important. Why should it be any different in the church?

In the church, leadership is a spiritual gift. Paul wrote, "He who exhorts, in exhortation; he who gives, with liberality; he who leads, with diligence" (Romans 12:8). That means God Himself calls and equips leaders within His church. Leadership isn't something to hide from or be embarrassed by, and it's definitely not something to boast about or abuse. Rather, leadership is to be used wisely and humbly, knowing that our gifts and calling are from God.

Dealing with Disorder

The church often struggles with chaos and confusion, but this is not a new problem. There was a lot of confusion and disorder in the church in Corinth, as well. Paul wrote 1 and 2 Corinthians to put the church in order. As I read the letters to the Corinthians, I see three things out of order in their church.

The first and most obvious was *the problem of sin.* "It is actually reported that there is sexual immorality among you, and such sexual immorality as is not even named among the Gentiles—that a man has his father's wife!" (1 Corinthians 5:1). In the debate about the new

Gentile converts in Acts 15, the apostles only had a few requirements for the new believers, and one of those was abstaining from sexual immorality. Immorality has destroyed so many believers and leaders. It not only damages others but is a sin against your own body. "Flee sexual immorality. Every sin that a man does is outside the body, but he who commits sexual immorality sins against his own body" (1 Corinthians 6:18).

I have seen churches on both sides of the pendulum, some liberal, others extremely legalistic, and they both have one thing in common: sin. The problem is not that there is sin in the House. "If anyone sins, we have an advocate with the Father" (1 John 2:1). The problem is when we hide our sin, ignore it, or deny it is there. "If we confess our sins, He is faithful and just to forgive us" (1 John 1:9), but "He who covers his sins will not prosper" (Proverbs 28:13). When we read 2 Corinthians, we see that the Corinthians repented and restored the church. We cannot ignore or tolerate sin.

The second problem in the Corinthian church was *the disorder regarding the gifts*

and manifestation of the Holy Spirit. If everyone speaks at the same time, it produces confusion. And if everyone speaks in tongues, but no
one interprets, there is no clear communication.
I am 100% full-gospel, charismatic, and baptized in the Holy Spirit. I believe the gifts of the

Holy Spirit are available for
us now, not that they were
just something from church
history whose time is past.
I speak in tongues, proph-
esy, receive and give words
of knowledge and wisdom,

The heart
behind
God's gifts
is always
to serve.

and am filled with the Holy Spirit every day. At
times people think I am a crazy Pentecostal,
and at other times people think I am limiting or
quenching the power of God.

Some interpret the order that we establish
in the House as "quenching" or stopping the
flow of the Holy Spirit. There is a big difference, however, between getting in the Spirit's
way and creating a safe environment to meet
God. Order in the House is what gives us the
freedom to worship, preach, care for children,
and more. This is not about controlling the

expression of anyone, but rather about serving everyone in a healthy way.

If someone insists on using their gift in a way that disrupts the work of the Spirit or makes people feel unsafe, it's not a "gift" at all. It's an interruption, an intrusion, and an imposition. Some people use the gifts of the Spirit to manipulate and control the church, and we cannot allow disorder in the House.

The heart behind God's gifts is always to serve. That means whoever wants to use their gifts must do so in a way that genuinely helps others.

The third problem in the church at Corinth was *the governance or leadership system.* Whenever we talk about order in the House, we come to the subject of leadership.

I remember the first time I visited England, back in the early 2000s. I had been given an incredible opportunity to attend a conference in a well-known church, and a friend of mine had even paid for my airfare. When I arrived, though, there was no one to pick me up. That was odd. Then, during the conference, it seemed like no one knew what to do or when to do it.

In the first session, a psychologist taught the "Healing Dance." The person explained that your body has memories like our brain. That's fine, I suppose—but the next step was to "dance out our healing" with this muscle memory. I told them I had two left feet and preferred to sit that one out. The second session was the "Healing Path," and it was also very subjective and odd.

The conference went through many sessions like this. I remember the feeling of chaos in each session as we listened to wave after wave of random, extreme, and strange doctrines. The worst part was that the supposed leader saw everything but just sat there and never led. I wanted to shout, "Hey, do something! Aren't you in charge?"

God established leaders for the church. "And He Himself gave some to be apostles, some prophets, some evangelists, and some pastors and teachers" (Ephesians 4:11). Passive, apathetic leaders are a big problem in the House. Someone must lead if structure and order are to exist. If leaders do not do their job, it produces disorder in the House.

Guard Your Heart

One reason I have found that leaders lose their confidence and stop leading is when they are hiding sin. They feel guilty or ashamed, but rather than fixing the problem and taking their place as leaders, they allow abuse and sin everywhere to go unchecked, producing disorder in the House.

A clear example of this in the Bible was Eli and his sons. Eli was the head priest, and his sons were responsible for the House of the Lord. However, they were vile men who raped the women and stole the sacrifices the people brought to offer to the Lord. Eli corrected them once, but he did not stop them, so God rebuked him. "Why do you kick at My sacrifice and My offering which I have commanded in My dwelling place, and honor your sons more than Me, to make yourselves fat with the best of all the offerings of Israel My people?" (1 Samuel 2:29). There was disorder in the House, and the leader did not exercise his authority.

I cannot tell you how many churches we destroy because the person called to lead

We need leaders who guide the church willingly, from the heart, as servant leaders who imitate Jesus. does not use their authority. We should never honor our natural or spiritual children more than the Lord. Because of a passive leader, Israel lost the glory of the Lord. That's why Eli's daughter-in-law named her child Ichabod, which means "no glory," and said, "The glory has departed from Israel!" (1 Samuel 4:21). The House deserves pastors who lay their lives down for the flock. We need leaders who guide the church willingly, from the heart, as servant leaders who imitate Jesus.

The Bible gives clear guidelines and limitations for pastors. "The elders who are among you I exhort, I who am a fellow elder and a witness of the sufferings of Christ, and also a partaker of the glory that will be revealed: Shepherd the flock of God which is among you, serving as overseers, not by compulsion but willingly, not for dishonest gain but eagerly;

nor as being lords over those entrusted to you, but being examples to the flock" (1 Peter 5:1–3).

Notice the boundaries and limits to pastoral authority in this passage. First and foremost, we must *guard our hearts*. We cannot allow the ministry to become an obligation or duty. If we allow people to pressure and manipulate us, we endanger our ability to serve from the heart. It can be all too easy to establish structures that turn heartfelt service into a legalistic obligation.

Another boundary that pastors have is *not doing things for dishonest gain*. In other words, the goal of our service shouldn't be to make more money. In Spanish, we have a little rhyme about the areas pastors tend to fail in: "La lana, la dama, y la fama." In English, that means "Money, women, and fame." That's not to say that finances, sex, or influence are the problem—the problem is that as leaders (both men and women), we too easily allow the temptations of the flesh to lead us astray.

Dishonest gain has taken down many church leaders. The moment I try to sell you a product or get something from you, I have crossed the boundary into dishonest gain. I destroy my eagerness to serve by my selfish motives. That is one reason I do not promote politics in the church. I am here to shepherd the flock of God, not gain votes.

The third clear limit in 1 Peter 5 is *not lording it over the church.* In church governance, we must make sure that we do not become lords in place of servant leaders. One of the dangers of denominational leadership is that organizations can try to control their congregants from afar by ordering a pastor to a different location, demoting those they dislike and promoting those they like, acting like little kings rather than being an example for the flock. We are not kings who shout from a distance but shepherds who lead from the front.

Church Government

As we have seen, order in the church starts with leadership. There are many systems or forms of church government that have been created to bring order to the House. While they all have their positive side, many also have negative sides. We need to be aware of the limitations of our church government structure and do our best to follow the New Testament model of church leadership.

Martin was a pastor in a sizeable main-line denomination, and over time, he rose to the level of bishop. Every July was a nightmare for Martin, though. That was when the general congress of the denomination would take place, and it was when pastors were assigned new churches. Time after time, after Martin and his family had fallen in love with a town and the people in the local church, the overseers of the denomination would decide it was time for them to move to a new church location. Martin would have to return home and inform his family that a group of people who didn't even know them had decided they must leave their friends and church family and move to a new town.

Frustrated, Martin decided to go independent. After getting to know each other for some years, Martin joined us in La Fuente. He now pastors La Fuente church in Mexicali on the USA border. The organization he was part of is run by a group of leaders, or bishops, who meet each year at a conference and make decisions for the local churches. This form of government is called *episcopal*.

Another form of government is called *congregational*. I remember awaiting the decision of a church with this type of government that was interested in supporting our orphanage in Tepic. My wife, Mary Jo, carries the fundraising burden for our two homes with thirty children. We needed the help, and the pastor was on board. He had a big heart for supporting the children. They had to put the decision to a churchwide vote, though. Finally, he told me, "Well, it was close. There were some unconvinced people, but in the end, you won." It must be very frustrating to be in a system of government that requires votes from the congregation, but that is what they do.

Jorge pastored a large church for thirty years. Seeing the need for more help, he hired a new pastor with a legal background. Soon afterward, he flew to several countries to preach and teach. Upon returning home after his long trip, Jorge went to the church and tried his key in the lock, but it didn't work. The locks had been changed. The new pastor accused Jorge of misusing funds and convinced the church board to lock him out.

After two long years of legal battles, Jorge lost all his retirement savings, church, and reputation. The church dwindled to ten percent of its original size, and people were scattered all over. What an extreme example of a board-driven church. In this form of leadership, people from all walks of life hold board meetings where they make significant decisions for the church. I always imagined Joe the plumber going to the Friday night board meeting after a long week of work. Should we add a service? Should we buy a new bus? Whatever the pastor asks, Joe answers no, because it is easier to say no than take responsibility for yes. I call it the ministry of no. Many churches I know use this form of government, which is called *presbyterian*.

Putting order in the House is not too complicated. We can simplify things by placing relationships above our methods and rules. I should never make decisions for people I do not even know. If we are so big that we can't develop authentic relationships from the heart, we need to put the House in order and put people above projects. If someone does not know and love the church, they definitely should not make life-changing decisions for her.

The best way to govern the church is to be led by the Spirit and use whatever organization He shows you. If the church already exists when you join, accept the form of government and work to improve it with prayer and service from the heart. It is your job to know the government of the organization you are part of and complement it, not complicate it.

All forms of church government have pros and cons, and your trust should be in God, not a leadership structure. Government and structure are necessary, though, which is why it's important to keep evaluating, learning, and improving. God has always worked through the limitation of human structures, and it's incredible what He accomplishes when we put people first and do our best to lead (and follow) wisely and faithfully.

CHAPTER NINE

PLANTING THE HOUSE

And the remnant who have escaped of the house of Judah shall again take root downward, and bear fruit upward.

—Isaiah 37:31

W̲E HAD JUST ARRIVED IN THE TINY TOWN OF SAN Ignacio, about ninety minutes outside Mazatlán, with a small team of Americans. This was the town where the police commander would be healed, but that was still in the future. This was 1992, and our goal was to find and support an existing church there. However, after driving through the entire town, we couldn't find any. I couldn't believe it. Mazatlán had many churches, but here, we could not find a single one.

San Ignacio was well known for its bugs, drugs, heat, and danger. It was common to hear about people losing friends and acquaintances to violence from drug trafficking. More than five thousand people lived in this place, but they had no church, no pastor, no worship, and no Christian fellowship. *Someone needs to start a church in this town,* I thought. And I felt the Lord ask me if I would. "Who will stay?" That was the question God was whispering in my heart.

This was long before we started La Fuente church in Tepic, back when I was in the process of leaving YWAM. Starting a church in such an unknown location would not be easy. There weren't many people who cared about the small town of San Ignacio. I knew I had to die to my idea of having a significant ministry and my dreams of future fame.

I decided to accept the challenge. Every Sunday, after three morning services at a church I was ministering at in Mazatlán, I would head out by myself to San Ignacio to begin planting the church. I quickly started to see some success. A young woman offered to let me hold services in her house, and soon after, about thirty youth were attending regularly. To see such fruit in a short amount of time was worth any struggle, and it was very encouraging.

Then things changed dramatically. As I traveled to San Ignacio one particular Sunday, my stomach ached and burned like crazy. I didn't think much of it, and I went to the home where we were meeting. Only three young people came to our service that week, so I asked the girl who let us use her home, "What is going on?" She told me that the Catholic priest had informed the people that I was evil and that they should not allow their children to attend the services. They accepted his instruction. After delivering the news, the young woman added, "Please don't ever come back to my home."

By the time I made it home that night, I had a high fever. I had typhoid! That same night I received a phone call from the United States. My main supporting church informed me that they were not happy with my work and would soon be reevaluating their financial support of my ministry.

In one day, life went from success to failure. I was without a church, without my health, and without financial support to continue. It was nothing close to what Job suffered, but I felt a bit like him—everything was gone in one day.

How to Fight Dragons

After taking some time to recuperate, my wife and I took a trip to visit churches and meet with our leading financial supporter, the one that was considering pulling the support. In one of the churches that we visited, a young man told me he had a vision of me, and he asked if he could share it. I felt extremely vulnerable, so I was hesitant to listen; but I was also too tired to resist, and I let him go ahead.

The young man told me that he saw me fighting a dragon on my own with just a spear in my hand. I had thrown my spear at the dragon, but it did nothing to harm it. Instead, the dragon turned toward me and burned me with fire from his mouth.

I thought, *if he is trying to encourage me, it is not working.* Nevertheless, I decided to keep listening.

He then said that he saw me return with an army, and together we conquered the dragon. I understood that our call to ministry was not a call to do it on our own. I learned then that my idea of the "lone missionary," the great man of

God who went out and made things happen through sheer grit and strength of character, was a bit unrealistic. The whole point is to get two or more together, to be a united body.

After returning from our trip, I began to gather every volunteer available to go with me and help me plant the House. When my Mexican friends go to the beach or drive into town, they bring everyone. Mom, dad, children, aunts, uncles, grandma, and the dog all hop in and enjoy the time together. That's how our church planting efforts were after that: everyone went together.

Now, when we plant churches, we always begin by gathering a great team. The more people there are, the better. We invite everyone who can come and serve. After planting churches for many years, God has blessed us with an incredible team. When we arrive in a city to plant a church, a pastor and a group of volunteers are always ready to help teach children, work with youth, and cover any need in the new church. Together we face the dragon, and together we defeat it. We storm the gates Hades, but they do not prevail against us.

The results that stem from teamwork are awesome. Hundreds of people gather in our services, volunteering and serving on the team. What one person cannot do alone, an excellent team can do together.

As I look at the church around the world, I see more and more pastors and youth stepping up to plant the House. And yet, so many try to fight the dragon alone. The gates of hell will not prevail against the church, but if you are not in the church, you are open to the dragon's attack. Even an all-star Christian is vulnerable without a brother or sister covering their back.

> What one person cannot do alone, an excellent team can do together.

I wish I could say that each church we have planted was the result of excellent planning and wise investment and that the work has always been easy, fun, and fulfilling. But that wouldn't be true. It has been tiring, at times, and even annoying, but it has also been glorious and satisfying. If it were easy to plant churches, there would already be one in every town. That is not the case, though. We know there will be trials and difficulties when we decide to plant a church, but it is worth it.

We consider a church planted when people are gathered together in His Name. "Those who are planted in the house of the LORD shall flourish in the courts of our God" (Psalm 92:13).

In other words, when people are planted in the church, the church is planted in the city. Sometimes we speak of planting churches, and other times we speak of people being planted in a local church. The two concepts work together, like two sides of the same coin.

Many want to flourish without being planted, but it doesn't work that way. A plant must have a root system or it will wither and die. In the same way, the House is the ground where people can grow roots for the Lord.

What does it look like to be planted in God's House? Here are a few characteristics common to those who are planted and flourishing in the House.

- They love other believers with fraternal love. Their best friends are in the House.

- They meet regularly. They don't give up meeting together as some do (Hebrews 10:25).
- They serve in the House. They use their talents and gifts to help others.
- They give to the House. They bring their tithe. Money and heart are connected (Matthew 6:21).

Keys to Church Planting

The job of planting the House is the work of gathering two or more people together who love God and love each other. Sometimes that can feel like herding cats or, as we say in Mexico, shepherding burros. We have learned a few things that work well in church planting, though.

First, as I said above, *we begin with a team.* We cannot kill the dragon alone. All church plants must start with a team. A struggling pastor once told me, "I don't have anyone capable of being on the team." I asked him, "What about your wife?" We must remember the most important members of the team: our families. If your wife and children are not with you, you do not have a team. "For if a man does not know how to rule his own house, how will he take care of the church of God?" (1 Timothy 3:5).

Second, *brotherly love among the church members* produces roots strong enough to resist the power of any storm. We can fight any battle and fix any problem if love is present because of unity's strong foundation.

> We can fight any battle and fix any problem if love is present.

Third, we plant the House with *major steps of faith*. We want to include three elements in every service that we have. First, consistent prayer times together; second, excellent praise and worship; and third, powerful preaching. By faith, we gather the team that we need to start, we train new leaders to fill each position, and we serve with all our strength.

Fourth, we make sure *the children's needs are met.* When we first started La Fuente in an upper room, space was very tight. But we eventually convinced the owner to rent us the lower floor, too. *Finally, I get offices.* These were my first thoughts. But as I considered how to build walls to make offices, a small voice reminded me of my own words: "What about the children?" I knew right then that my office would have to wait. The church is for the new generation, and children's ministry is a priority.

It's a good thing I decided to use that space for children because the kids quickly outgrew the space, and they dragged along their reluctant parents, who then became happy members, which grew our church. When we plant a church, we always ask, "What about the children?" Our team that works with La Fuente's kids is considered one of Mexico's most influential children's ministries.

Fifth, a House needs *a location.* The building where the church gathers is not holy or sacred, but without a building, we cannot rest and grow in a healthy environment. On the other hand, when peace and security are present, a church can flourish.

Our goal is for each church to have its

own land and building where it can grow. We work to have everything in order legally, economically, and spiritually for that to happen. If there is no building suitable for the House, then that becomes our first goal as a church. We plant the House with a minimum of two weekly services, and we *never* cancel. Consistency is key during the planting season. We strive to do our best in every service, every time we meet together.

How about you? Are you planted in the House of God? Are you flourishing there, with roots going down deep into God's love and truth?

Beyond that, are you committed to helping plant the House in places where it does not yet exist? All of us share the mission Jesus gave us: to go to the entire world and make disciples; to go to every city, town, village, and neighborhood to plant the House of God, and to help people become planted in the House of God.

Whether your role is to go or stay, to give or pray, to encourage or visit, there is always more to do to see God's House planted around the world.

CHAPTER TEN

HOMESICK

How lovely is Your tabernacle, O LORD of hosts! My soul longs, yes, even faints for the courts of the LORD; My heart and my flesh cry out for the living God. Even the sparrow has found a home, and the swallow a nest for herself, where she may lay her young— Even Your altars, O LORD of hosts, my King and my God.

—Psalm 84:1-3

A S A YOUNG MAN, I WAS OFTEN IN TROUBLE. I WAS even sent to juvenile jail for seven months. I stole, tried every drug I could find, fought, and was immoral with girls. I disappointed and broke my father's heart over and over again.

Once I became a Christian, my dad and I grew closer than ever before. Dad had always been kind and funny, but my sin and foolishness produced a separation that only Christ could repair.

I remember my baptism. I was standing with my pastor in a pool in front of our congregation. My father stood up in front of everyone and asked to speak, a request the pastor gladly accepted. Then, with everyone watching, my dad began crying. He said, "I am so proud of my son and thankful to Jesus for saving him and answering our prayers."

What could I say? In front of everyone, my dad was crying and embarrassing me! Then, of course, I cried, too. I went under the water full of love for my God and my parents.

It cost them everything to provide a home for us. My mother spent many nights agonizing in prayer for us while dad worked the night shift. We did not have much, but we had what we needed. So many times, people told them to apply tough love and kick me out of the house. But they always persevered and never stopped loving me.

I still have the picture of my dad fake-choking me in front of my '57 Chevy pickup as I said goodbye and headed out for missionary training school. I was immediately hit with a bad case of homesickness. I know it was not very "tough and independent," but I could not help the feelings of nostalgia and sadness that washed over me. Tears rolled down my cheeks as I drove south on the freeway. I knew I would not be back to live there again, and I cried like a little child, alone in that truck, missing my home's warmth and care.

There is something about "coming home" that is built into the human heart. We were created to be at home. To be in a family. To be safe, provided for, cared for, and loved. When home is missing, our hearts can tell.

Zeal for the House

Of course, many people have never had a home to miss. The idea of homesickness is entirely foreign to some. As we work with orphans in our children's homes in Tepic, we constantly battle detachment problems. Many of them cannot understand what it is like to have a loving, safe home. Some children even make themselves hard to love by insulting, cursing, and hitting the staff. They need to learn that they are accepted in Jesus.

God made us accepted in the beloved. "Now, therefore, you are no longer strangers and foreigners, but fellow citizens with the saints and members of the household of God" (Ephesians 2:19). God adopted us into His family and made us members of His household, His church. Because of His unconditional love, He made a place for us. We find a family and a loving home environment in the church.

It is hard to miss your church home if you never had one. Unfortunately, many local churches are less like homes and more like social clubs or prisons. The members are not children but enslaved people obligated to fulfill their spiritual duty. The pastors are not servant leaders but controlling warlords ruling over the flock. No wonder people don't feel homesick when they leave. Instead of homesickness, they are sick of their home. They experience relief when they get out from under that condemning, controlling atmosphere.

God doesn't want His House to be a place of abuse, but rather one of love, prayer, and family. Whip in hand, Jesus cleansed the temple and drove out those who bought and sold in it, saying, "It is written, 'My house is a house of prayer,' but you have made it a 'den of thieves'" (Luke 19:46). John added, "Then His disciples remembered that it was written, 'Zeal for Your house has eaten Me up'" (John 2:17). Jesus showed us genuine zeal for the House. In a sense, He was showing us His homesickness. He longed for the House to be what God had made it to be.

We feel a consuming ache when the House has been corrupted and no longer functions as His body.

Similarly, we feel a consuming ache when the House has been corrupted and no longer functions as His body. It is a longing for the courts of the Lord, for the pure presence of God, for the atmosphere of love and peace that God's throne of grace provides for us. That is the opposite of the money changers, with their corruption and abuse. Their only goal was to make money off the people who brought their sacrifices to the temple.

Back when I had only been a Christian for

three months, Brad, Carol, and I started going everywhere together. I think Carol liked Brad, but I just wanted to be with other Christian friends and get to know the Lord. So when someone invited us to see an evangelist from Texas in the Elk Lodge downtown, we jumped at the opportunity.

When we arrived at the door, they asked our names, where we lived, and what we did. Inside, the place seemed weird to me. The hosts got the crowd excited with a dramatic introduction of "the great evangelist" who was here to minister. When he arrived on the scene, he had big hair, flashy clothes, and giant rings on several fingers. He said that he had fasted and prayed over forty Bibles for forty days and that forty people were going to give four hundred dollars per Bible. That was the offering, he explained.

I did the math: sixteen thousand dollars. It was 1980, so that was an enormous amount of money. Then he turned our way, and with fiery eyes, he looked at Brad and called him by name, adding where he was from and what he did for a living. That blew Brad away. How did the evangelist know so much about him? I guess Brad forgot they asked us all that information when we arrived.

The guy was a fraud, a charlatan, and a thief. Even after selling the forty Bibles and saying that it was the only offering he would ask for, he proceeded to ask for another. Everyone had to get up and march in front of the entire room to give. I stayed in my seat, embarrassed but determined not to give him a penny. That was the first time I felt this homesickness, this zeal for His House. I felt like getting a whip and driving that guy out of town, big hair and all.

Brad gave a significant offering. Once we were in the car, I reminded him that they asked us for our personal information when we arrived. Brad just slumped down in his seat and moaned. What a waste. What a shame.

Too many false prophets have turned God's House into a den of thieves. The apostle Paul had the same concern about false teachers. "For I know this, that after my departure savage wolves will come in among you, not sparing the flock" (Acts 20:29). Is it wrong for us to fiercely protect the House after all the prayer, blood, sweat, toil, and tears we have invested? I, for one, will not simply let wolves come in and devour the flock.

No Place Like Home

In Mexico, there is something almost sacred about a mother. Mary, the mother of Jesus, is highly revered, and motherhood in general is a symbol of unconditional love, faithfulness, and presence. For many Mexicans, it was their mothers who nourished, comforted, and guided their children while the fathers were away working (or maybe absent from the home). That is why, in our culture here, you don't insult or offend someone's mother. Or, if you want to make someone really angry, use their mother in some creative combination with a swear word! I believe all of us have a deep longing for the comfort and care of our mother and home. It is this homesickness we constantly feel. We can think of the first mother, Eve; the second mother, Mary; and the third, the church, the bride of Christ.

I think many of us suffer from undiagnosed homesickness. The desire for home is there, but we have not correctly identified the source of our restlessness and longing. Like Abraham, we left our homeland, looking for a new country. "He waited for the city which has foundations, whose builder and maker is God" (Hebrews 11:10). Deep inside each of us is a desire to be in perfect union with Christ, to find that home that God has built for us.

We will never feel completely at home on earth, but the closest we can be is when we form part of the Body of Christ. When we are in one accord in His name, He fills the House, and it becomes a taste of heaven on earth. In His House, we find the answer to our longing for heaven.

I love how Psalm 84 describes the House of God. It starts by saying, "My soul longs, yes, even faints for the courts of the Lord" (verse 2). That is the cry of a homesick soul. The Psalm then describes in poetic fashion our journey to meet with God. "They go from strength to strength; Each one appears before God in Zion" (Psalm 84:7). The verse just before that refers to the Valley of Baca, which means the Valley of Weeping. In other words, even though we face pain and tears in life, we find strength as we pursue God. Then, in verse 10, the psalmist writes: "For a day in Your courts is better than a thousand. I would rather be a doorkeeper in the house of my God Than dwell in the tents of wickedness." Can you hear the passion in his voice to do whatever it takes, to pay whatever price, just to be close to God? That is the homesick cry of the heart, and it finds its home in the House.

> There is no place like home, and we are home when we are in the church.

The Psalm leaves no doubt that we are on a journey to reunite with Christ in His House. The purpose of this life is not just to survive. It is to be joined with God in perfect love in heaven. Meanwhile, we have a piece of heaven here with us: the church. There is no place like home, and we are home when we are in the church.

When I see the dangers and the attacks the church faces, something rises within me. It's homesickness. It's a zeal for His House that consumes me. No, the church isn't perfect. But she is beautiful. And she is called and designed by God to be a refuge for a world that is trying to find its way home.

That's why we must work harder than ever. The House is too important to be abandoned, but we cannot let it become something else than what it was designed to be. We must not allow false prophets or winds of doctrine to blow us off course. We cannot permit abusive, self-serving leaders to hurt people. We can never become simply another business or corporate endeavor. We should not use the House to attack and compete with others. We must never turn it into some political tool or power base. None of those things will produce the House that Jesus is building.

I know that some people find it easy to rip on the House, but they don't realize what they are damaging. The answer isn't to destroy the

House that Jesus is building, but rather to build it the way Jesus wants so that it can be a House of prayer for all nations, where all are welcome and all are safe.

The House, as we have seen, is more than just a human idea or endeavor. It is a spiritual creation. Something new and divine is born when we are gathered together in His name.

Do you remember what Jesus prayed? "That they all may be one, as You, Father, are in Me, and I in You; that they also may be one in Us, that the world may believe that You sent Me" (John 17:21).

That prayer is being answered today by people all over the world. This spiritual creation, this building of living stones, this glorious bride, this carefully constructed House—it's what Jesus is building.

He is building His House throughout the whole earth. And wherever He builds it, He asks the same question.

"Who will stay?"

ABOUT THE AUTHOR

Dwight Wesley Hansen and his wife, Mary Jo, have been missionaries to Mexico since 1988, and they are the founding pastors of *La Fuente Ministries*. Dwight is the director of *Heart4Mexico*, a nonprofit in the USA, and Mary Jo is the director of *Nana's House* orphanage. Dwight ministers frequently in the churches in La Fuente's network as well as many churches and conferences worldwide. He is the author of three books in Spanish. *Who Will Stay?* is his first book in English. Dwight loves building all kinds of things, but above all, he loves building churches. Dwight and Mary Jo live in Tepic, Nayarit, close to their two children and their grandson.

Made in USA - Kendallville, IN
12520_9781949791709
09.16.2022 1524